Social Issues
in Literature

Genocide in
Anne Frank's
The Diary of a Young Girl

Other Books in the Social Issues in Literature Series:

Social Issues in Literature

Genocide in Anne Frank's *The Diary of a Young Girl*

Louise Hawker, Book Editor

GREENHAVEN PRESS
A part of Gale, Cengage Learning

GALE
CENGAGE Learning

Detroit • New York • San Francisco • New Haven, Conn • Waterville, Maine • London

Elizabeth Des Chenes, *Managing Editor*

© 2012 Greenhaven Press, a part of Gale, Cengage Learning

Gale and Greenhaven Press are registered trademarks used herein under license.

For more information, contact:
Greenhaven Press
27500 Drake Rd.
Farmington Hills, MI 48331-3535
Or you can visit our Internet site at gale.cengage.com

For product information and technology assistance, contact us at

Gale Customer Support, 1-800-877-4253
For permission to use material from this text or product, submit all requests online at www.cengage.com/permissions

Further permissions questions can be emailed to permissionrequest@cengage.com

Articles in Greenhaven Press anthologies are often edited for length to meet page requirements. In addition, original titles of these works are changed to clearly present the main thesis and to explicitly indicate the author's opinion. Every effort is made to ensure that Greenhaven Press accurately reflects the original intent of the authors. Every effort has been made to trace the owners of copyrighted material.

Cover photograph copyright © Everett Collection Inc/Alamy.

LIBRARY OF CONGRESS CATALOGING-IN-PUBLICATION DATA

Genocide in Anne Frank's the Diary of a young girl / Louise Hawker, book editor.
  p. cm. -- (Social issues in literature)
  Includes bibliographical references and index.
  ISBN 978-0-7377-5448-3 (hardcover) -- ISBN 978-0-7377-5449-0 (pbk.)
  1. Holocaust, Jewish (1939-1945)--Netherlands--Amsterdam--Influence. 2. Frank, Anne, 1929-1945--Influence. 3. Frank, Anne, 1929-1945. Achterhuis--History and criticism. 4. Genocide--Sociological aspects. I. Hawker, Louise.
  DS135.N4G38 2011
  940.53'18092--dc22
                                                        2011009382

Printed in the United States of America
1 2 3 4 5 6 7 15 14 13 12 11

Contents

Anne Frank died of typhoid fever and malnutrition in
the Bergen-Belsen concentration camp in 1945 at age fifteen. But her talent as a writer, awareness of her emerg-
ing womanhood, and skill for self-analysis have continued to inspire readers since the diary was originally
published in English in 1952 as *Anne Frank: The Diary of
a Young Girl*. Anne's potential is evident in her diary's insightful descriptions of daily life in the Annex where she
and her family hid from the Nazis for two years before
their eventual capture.

After discovering the existence of Anne's diary, her father,
Otto Frank, was torn about publishing it in its entirety.
He has been criticized for editing the original and the
for-publication versions, both unfinished; however, Anne
herself had begun rewriting her diary for eventual publication, and she herself edited out references to sexuality
and criticism of her mother.

Miep Gies, one of Otto Frank's employees, played a pivotal role in providing for the safety of the Franks during
their time in the Annex. At her own peril, Gies saved
Anne's diary and writings after the Nazis found the
Franks and took them away to the concentration camps.

Women who were imprisoned in the Bergen-Belsen concentration camp with Anne and her sister recount Anne's last days and her death.

Chapter 2: *The Diary of a Young Girl* and Genocide

Anne Frank's diary is replete with images and references to hiding, both in the physical realm of the Annex and in the perspectives of Anne the writer. The residents of the Annex develop their own secret inner lives as they become invisible to the world in their efforts to survive annihilation.

Anne Frank's diary demonstrated the importance of women's and even children's writing outside the traditionally accepted literary boundaries. People around the world could identify with her insights and come to terms with her identity and struggles.

Elie Wiesel's story, that of a survivor, is part of the grand narrative of males who were arrested, deported, and sent to concentration camps. Anne Frank's story is a voice that speaks for the six million who vanished.

Anne Frank's sentiments about people trivialized the actual experience and fear of the Jews' hidden life and elevated Anne to a legend. In actuality, many of the Dutch were indifferent to the suffering and disappearance of the Jews in their midst.

Chapter 3: Contemporary Perspectives on Genocide

Mining for aluminum in India displaces indigenous people, killing their culture and destroying their land and social structure.

When Rwanda's genocide ended in 1994, three hundred thousand children had been murdered and ninety-five thousand had been orphaned. Ten years later, children were still suffering the consequences, including having to act as heads of households.

Introduction

It is said that Anne Frank's *The Diary of a Young Girl* is the second most read book in the world after the Bible. Whether that statement is fact or fiction, the continuing popularity of a small diary written by a teenager more than half a century ago cannot be disputed. Ellen Feldman, writing in the *American Heritage Magazine*'s February/March 2005 issue, states that the diary has been translated into fifty-five languages and sold more than 24 million copies. These staggering numbers are far beyond the readership young Anne envisioned when she began revising her diary for eventual publication. If nothing else, Anne's gifts as a writer have, sadly, brought her the recognition she dreamed of during her two years of hiding in the secret Annex. And for many readers, the diary is their first, and perhaps only, introduction to the Holocaust.

But *The Diary of A Young Girl* has also been a lightning rod for those who would use it and recraft it—as well as for those who wished to suppress the horrific segment of history it represents. Writing in *The Hidden Life of Otto Frank*, Carol Ann Lee observes, "Perhaps Otto would have been less keen to allow alterations to his daughter's diary if he had known the results of polls conducted in Germany. In October 1948, 41 percent of Germans still approved of the Nazi seizure of power. In 1952, 37 percent felt it was better for Germany not to have any Jews, and in the same year, 88 percent said they felt no personal responsibility for the mass exterminations." The reaction to the German edition of Anne's diary was, not surprisingly, tepid.

Shocking as those statistics are, other nations and peoples were also eager to put World War II and the Nazi atrocities behind them. In the 1950s, after the years of war-caused stress and shortages, Americans embraced complacency, conformity, and their newfound materialism. At the same time, a number of European populations, such as the French and the Dutch, also wished to minimize their roles in allowing the Nazis to terrorize, deport and kill their Jewish neighbors and citizens.

In spite of these obstacles, *The Diary of a Young Girl* was published in English in the United States in 1952. When a rave review of the diary, by Meyer Levin, appeared on the front page of the *New York Times Book Review* on June 15, 1952, the first edition of the book sold out, and additional printings were soon under way. Levin evolved into a key player in the promotion and reappropriation of the diary. As a war correspondent, he had seen firsthand the stacked bodies and the starving, sick survivors of the death camps. He became, by his own admission, obsessed with the diary and with producing a dramatic play of the story. Levin and Otto Frank engaged in nearly two decades of lawsuits and countersuits about his play, which was never produced. Eventually, the play was written by two non-Jewish playwrights, and it opened in 1955 to accolades, going on to win the Pulitzer Prize as well as a Tony Award.

But controversy continued to follow Anne's diary. Relatives of the dentist Dussel, whose real name was Fritz Pfeffer, charged that in the stage play he was inaccurately portrayed as an ignorant buffoon, a slur on his character. A fictitious scene inserted in the play in which Mr. Van Daan stole bread from the communal cupboard also defamed, according to survivors, the memory of the real man, Hermann van Pels. A subsequent movie version was called, by some critics, a sugar-coated portrayal of the real and omnipresent terror of daily life in the Annex. In fact, when the original cut of the movie was previewed, it included scenes of Anne at Auschwitz. Audiences angrily noted their disapproval on their rating cards. This information, they felt, was in conflict with the upbeat, happy Anne they wanted to know.

As these events illustrate, Anne Frank's diary has often been used to promote individual aspirations and purposes. In a 1997 article in the *New Yorker* titled "Who Owns Anne Frank?" novelist and critic Cynthia Ozick stated that the diary had been misunderstood and misrepresented, even by its greatest supporters. Ozick went so far as to say, "But one can imagine a still more salvational outcome: Anne Frank's diary burned, vanished, lost—saved from a world that made of it all things, some of them true, while floating lightly over the heavier truth of named and inhabited evil."

Many others, however, view the diary as a critical document that personalizes the plight of 6 million Jews who died in the Holocaust. They argue that with continuing interest in her diary, Anne Frank's voice resonates through the decades as a reminder of the worst, and most inhumanely destructive, era of modern history. The essays in *Social Issues in Literature: Genocide in Anne Frank's* The Diary of a Young Girl examine the book's significance as a Holocaust document as well as viewpoints on genocide in the twenty-first century.

Chronology

February 16, 1926
Margot Frank, Anne's sister, is born in Frankfurt, Germany, to Otto and Edith Frank. The Franks are Germans of Jewish descent.

June 12, 1929
Anne Frank is born in Frankfurt, Germany.

Summer 1933
Edith, Margot, and Anne move to Aachen, Germany, to stay with the girls' grandmother.

September 15, 1933
Otto Frank founds a business in Amsterdam, where he had existing business connections.

December 5, 1933
Edith and Margot leave Aachen and move to Amsterdam.

February 1934
Anne arrives in Amsterdam and joins her family after staying with her grandmother in Aachen. She is enrolled in a Montessori school.

May 10, 1940
Germany invades the Netherlands.

Fall 1941
Jewish children are forced to leave Dutch schools and attend segregated Jewish schools in Amsterdam.

June 12, 1942
Anne receives a diary for her birthday.

July 5, 1942

Margot receives a notice to report for deportation to a labor camp.

July 6, 1942

The Frank family goes into hiding in the Annex above Otto Frank's business at 263 Prinsengracht Street.

July 13, 1942

The van Pels family (known as the van Daans family in Anne's diary) join the Franks in hiding.

November 16, 1942

Fritz Pfeffer (known as Mr. Dussel in Anne's diary) joins the Franks and the van Pelses as the eighth person in hiding in the Annex.

March 1944

Anne hears the Netherlands government-in-exile on the radio asking people to retain their memoirs for postwar publication. Anne begins to rewrite portions of her diary for eventual publication.

August 1, 1944

Anne Frank makes the last entry in her diary.

August 4, 1944

The residents of the Annex are arrested by the Dutch Nazis and eventually taken to Westerbork, a transit camp in northeastern Holland.

August 5, 1944

Miep Gies, a secretary in Otto Frank's business, discovers and hides Anne's diary from the Nazis.

September 3, 1944
The residents of the Annex are transported in a sealed cattle car to the Auschwitz concentration camp. There, the men and women are separated.

October 1944
Anne, Margot, and Mrs. van Pels are transferred to the Bergen-Belsen concentration camp. Edith Frank remains at Auschwitz in the women's section.

January 6, 1945
Edith Frank dies at Auschwitz.

January 27, 1945
The Russian army liberates Auschwitz, and Otto Frank, who is barely alive, is set free.

March 1945
Margot Frank dies in the Bergen-Belsen concentration camp; Anne Frank, age fifteen, dies a few days later. Both girls suffered from typhoid fever and starvation.

April 15, 1945
Bergen-Belsen is liberated by British soldiers.

June 1945
Otto Frank returns to Amsterdam and lives with Miep Gies and her husband, Jan. He knows his wife is dead but does not know the fate of Anne and Margot.

October 24, 1945
Otto Frank receives confirmation that Margot and Anne are dead. Now knowing Anne will not return, Miep Gies gives Anne's diary to Otto.

1947
Anne Frank's diary is published in Holland.

1952

Anne's diary is published in the United States.

October 5, 1955

The play *The Diary of Anne Frank* opens in New York and later wins a Tony Award and the Pulitzer Prize.

1957

Otto Frank and others establish the Anne Frank Foundation to preserve the building where the group hid from the Nazis and eventually open it to the public.

1959

The movie version of *The Diary of Anne Frank* opens in US movie theaters.

May 3, 1960

The Anne Frank House opens to the public and the Anne Frank Foundation launches a campaign against bigotry and hatred.

1963

Nazi hunter Simon Wiesenthal captures the man who arrested Anne Frank, Karl Silberbauer.

1977

The Anne Frank Center USA is founded in the United States to promote a universal message of tolerance through education and events.

August 19, 1980

Otto Frank dies and wills Anne's diary to the Netherlands Institute for War Documentation.

1986

The Netherlands Institute for War Documentation commissions a forensic analysis of the diary to determine its authenticity, in the wake of claims of forgery by Holocaust deniers and others. The diary is determined to be authentic.

June 1986

The Diary of Anne Frank: The Critical Edition is published in Dutch.

March 1995

The Diary of a Young Girl: The Definitive Edition is published in English.

June 1995

The documentary film *Anne Frank Remembered* premieres and wins an Academy Award.

2003

The US Holocaust Memorial Museum mounts an Anne Frank exhibition, including a display of her original writings, in connection with the museum's tenth anniversary.

January 11, 2010

Miep Gies dies at age one hundred.

August 23, 2010

The chestnut tree that Anne Frank wrote about in her diary, now known as the Anne Frank tree, topples in a windstorm.

Social Issues
in Literature

CHAPTER 1

Background on
Anne Frank

The Life of Anne Frank

Contemporary Authors Online

Contemporary Authors Online is a web-based reference work published by Gale Cengage Learning.

This biographical summary of Anne Frank's life focuses on the period after the family moved from Frankfurt, Germany, to Amsterdam, the Netherlands. Anne's potential for becoming a notable writer is evident in her insightful descriptions of daily life, her ability for self-analysis, and the people with whom she shared the Annex for two years before capture by the Nazis. Anne died in the Bergen-Belsen concentration camp in 1945, one month before its liberation by the Allies. Her spirit and chronicles, however, have inspired readers since the diary was published in English in 1952.

Anne Frank, a victim of the Holocaust during World War II, became known throughout the world through her eloquent diary, describing the two years she and seven others hid from Nazis in an attic above her father's business office in Amsterdam. In the diary Anne relates the fear of being discovered and the aggravations of life in hiding as well as the feelings and experiences of adolescence that are recognized by people everywhere. Anne received the first notebook as a present from her parents on her thirteenth birthday in 1942, about a month before the family went into hiding. She wrote in the diary until the discovery of the hiding place in August, 1944. Anne's father, Otto Frank, the only one of them to survive the concentration camps to which they were sent, agreed to publish the diary in 1946.

Contemporary Authors Online, "Anne(lies) (Marie) Frank," 2003. Copyright © Gale, a part of Cengage Learning, Inc. Reproduced by permission.

Anne Sees Her Diary as a Friend

The Franks moved from Frankfurt, Germany—where Anne was born—to Amsterdam in 1933 after Germany ruled that Jewish and German children had to attend segregated schools. In July, 1942, after Anne's sister Margot received notice to report to the Dutch Nazi organization, the Franks immediately went into hiding in the "Secret Annex," as Anne dubbed the attic of the Amsterdam warehouse. Soon after, Mr. and Mrs. Frank and their two girls welcomed Mr. and Mrs. Van Daan (pseudonymous names used by Anne) and their son Peter into their rooms, and lastly Mr. Dussel, an elderly dentist. In an entry about her family's flight into hiding, Anne wrote that the diary was the first thing she packed. It meant a great deal to her; she viewed the diary as a personal friend and confidant, as she remarked June 20, 1942, in a reflection about the diary itself: "I haven't written for a few days, because I wanted first of all to think about my diary. It's an odd idea for someone like me to keep a diary; not only because I have never done so before, but because it seems to me that neither I—nor for that matter anyone else—will be interested in the unbosomings of a thirteen-year-old schoolgirl. Still, what does that matter? I want to write, but more than that, I want to bring out all kinds of things that lie buried deep in my heart. . . . [T]here is no doubt that paper is patient and as I don't intend to show this . . . 'diary' to anyone, unless I find a real friend, boy or girl, probably nobody cares. And now I come to the root of the matter, the reason for my starting a diary; it is that I have no such real friend. . . . [I]t's the same with all my friends, just fun and joking, nothing more. I can never bring myself to talk of anything outside the common round. . . . Hence, this diary. . . . I don't want to set down a series of bald facts in a diary as most people do, but I want this diary itself to be my friend, and I shall call my friend Kitty." . . .

Apart from interest in the diary for its historical value and for the extreme circumstances under which it was written, some have admired the diary for its accurate, revealing portrait of adolescence. "She described life in the 'Annex' with all its inevitable tensions and quarrels," wrote L. De Jong in *A Tribute to Anne Frank*. "But she created first and foremost a wonderfully delicate record of adolescence, sketching with complete honesty a young girl's feelings, her longings and loneliness."

Anne Struggled with Adolescent Emotions

At the age of thirteen, when Anne began the diary, she was struggling with the problems of growing up. Lively and vivacious, she was chastised at school—and later in the annex—for her incessant chattering. In the annex she was forced to whisper throughout the day. It was a great trial for Anne, who wrote on October 1, 1942, "We are as quiet as mice. Who, three months ago, would ever have guessed that quicksilver Anne would have to sit still for hours—and, what's more—could?" After a year of this silence, combined with confinement indoors, she expressed her feelings of depression, writing on October 29, 1943, "The atmosphere is so oppressive, and sleepy and as heavy as lead. You don't hear a single bird singing outside, and a deadly close silence hangs everywhere, catching hold of me as if it will drag me down deep into an underworld. . . . I wander from one room to another, downstairs and up again, feeling like a songbird whose wings have been clipped and who is hurling himself in utter darkness against the bars of his cage."

Seclusion Bred Tension in the Annex

The eight people lived in constant fear of being discovered. Their concerns were heightened by seeing and hearing about other Jews who were rounded up in Amsterdam, and by burglars at the warehouse who threatened to find them accidentally. These fears, in addition to the stress of close confinement, resulted in great tension and many quarrels. Anne could be headstrong, opinionated, and critical—especially of her mother. Generally cheerful and optimistic, she adored her father and attempted to get along with the others, but she was sensitive to criticism, explaining in her diary that no one criticized her more than she herself. The diary thus traces her development from an outgoing, popular child to an introspective, idealistic young woman. Her entry on July 11, 1943, illustrates her developing tact: "I do really see that I get on better by shamming a bit, instead of my old habit of telling everyone exactly what I think." Anne herself described the two sides of her personality in her final entry: "I have, as it were, a dual personality. One half embodies my exuberant cheerfulness, making fun of everything, my high-spiritedness, and above all, the way I take everything lightly. . . . This side is usually lying in wait and pushes away the other, which is much better, deeper and purer."

Anne's Writing Shows Ability for Self-Analysis

It is this introspection and ability to express her various moods that distinguishes her diary, [Henry F.] Pommer noted [in a 1960 essay]: "Any diary of a young girl who hid in Amsterdam during the Nazi occupation, who described her first protracted love affair, and who was a person of breeding, humor, religious sensitivity, and courage might well interest us. But Anne had one further trait of the utmost importance for her own maturity and for what she wrote: an unusual ability for self-analysis. She knew she had moods, and she could write eloquently about them—about loneliness for example. But she could also step outside her moods in order to evaluate them."

Her friend Lies Goslar later attributed Anne's rapid maturity to the many hours of quiet reflection encouraged by hiding, the severity of her situation, and her tender relationship with Peter Van Daan. A former teacher expressed surprise at the transformation in her character and writing because Anne

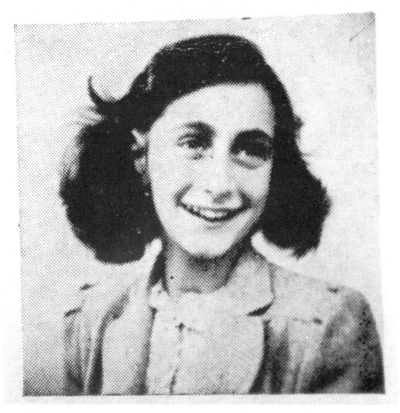

A *photograph of Anne Frank, author of* The Diary of a Young Girl, *taken in May 1942.* © EPA/Anita Maric/Landov.

had not been an exceptional student. Even Anne's father admitted, "I never knew my little Anna was so deep." She meditated on religion, developed a strong sense of morality, and deliberately set about improving her own character. On July 15, 1944, she wrote: "It's really a wonder that I haven't dropped all my ideals, because they seem so absurd and impossible to carry out. . . . I simply can't build up my hopes on a foundation consisting of confusion, misery and death. I see the world gradually being turned into a wilderness, I hear the ever approaching thunder, which will destroy us too, I can feel the sufferings of millions and yet, if I look up into the heavens, I think that it will all come right, that this cruelty too will end, and that peace and tranquility will return again. . . . In the meantime, I must uphold my ideals, for perhaps the time will come when I shall be able to carry them out." She vowed to make a difference, writing on April 6, 1944: "I know what I want, I have a goal, an opinion, I have a religion and love. . . . I know that I'm a woman, a woman with inward strength and plenty of courage. If God lets me live . . . I shall not remain insignificant, I shall work in the world and for mankind!"

Anne Decides to Be a Writer

During the course of writing the diary, Anne became certain she wanted to be a writer. She envisioned a novel based on her diary. Additionally she wrote stories, later collected in *The Works of Anne Frank* and *Tales From the House Behind*. According to *New York Times Book Review* critic Frederick Morton, the stories "show that Anne followed instinctively the best of all platitudes: Write whereof you know. Not even her little fairy tales are easy escapes into make-believe, but rather pointed allegories of reality—the two elves who are imprisoned together to learn tolerance; or Blurry the Baby who runs away from home to find the great, free, open world, and never does. . . . Still none of these . . . , not even a charming little morality tale like 'The Wise Old Dwarf,' has the power of any single entry in the diary."

Anne's Diary Ends Before Her Arrest

The diary ends August 1, 1944, three days before the group was arrested and sent to the concentration camp at Auschwitz, Poland. Carol Ann Lee, author of *The Hidden Life of Otto Frank*, asserts that Otto Frank's business associate Anton Ahlers is responsible for alerting Nazi authorities to the hiding place of the Frank family in 1944. Nazis raided the Amsterdam annex after an anonymous phone call, and the identity of the caller has never been definitively revealed. The family was separated, and Margot and Anne were later transferred to

Bergen-Belsen. According to a survivor who knew her at the concentration camp, Anne never lost her courage, deep sensitivity, or ability to feel. An excerpt of Ernst Schnabel's *Anne Frank: A Portrait in Courage*, reprinted in *A Tribute to Anne Frank*, states that "Anne was the youngest in her group, but nevertheless she was the leader of it. She also distributed the bread in the barracks, and she did it so well and fairly that there was none of the usual grumbling. . . . Here is another example. We were always thirsty. . . . And once, when I was so far gone that I almost died because there was nothing to drink, Anne suddenly came to me with a cup of coffee. To this day I don't know where she got it." The woman continued: "She, too, was the one who saw to the last what was going on all around us. . . . We were beyond feelings. . . . Something protected us, kept us from seeing. But Anne had no such protection, to the last. I can still see her standing at the door and looking down the camp street as a herd of naked gypsy girls was driven by, to the crematory, and Anne watched them going and cried. And she cried also when we marched past the Hungarian children who had already been waiting half a day in the rain in front of the gas chambers, because it was not yet their turn. And Anne nudged me and said: 'Look, look. Their eyes. . . . '"

Both Anne and Margot died of typhoid fever at Bergen-Belsen in March, 1945. Their mother had died earlier at Auschwitz. Otto Frank, liberated from Auschwitz by Russian troops in 1945, returned to Amsterdam. He already knew of his wife's death, but he had hope that Margot and Anne were alive. He soon received a letter informing him of their deaths. It was then that Miep Gies, who had worked for Mr. Frank as a secretary and helped hide the family, gave Anne's writings to him. Gies had discovered the diaries strewn on the floor after the Franks' arrest, and she kept the writings at her home but did not read them. It took Anne's father several weeks to read the diary as he could only bear to read a little at a time. Urged by friends, he published an edited version of the diary, deleting a number of passages he thought too personal.

Fifty years after the diary was first published, a new edition was published that included the passages Otto had originally deleted.

The Anne Frank Foundation has preserved the Franks' hiding place in Amsterdam, and schools in several countries, as well as a village at Wuppertal, West Germany, have been named for Anne.

Anne Revised Her Diary with Plans for Publication

Carol Ann Lee

Carol Ann Lee has authored several books about Anne Frank, including Roses from the Earth: The Biography of Anne Frank. *She has also written three children's books about Frank.*

Lee states that Frank's father, Otto, was torn about publishing the diary in total due to what he considered sensitive or extremely personal descriptions of sexuality and criticism of her mother. Otto was widely criticized for editing out such passages in the original versions of the diary. Anne had, however, already begun rewriting some passages with the intent of eventual publication, spurred on by a speech by the ruler of the Netherlands government in exile, stating that journals and diaries of the period would be valuable once the war was over.

Asked years later about his editing of the diary, Otto [Frank] replied: "Of course Anne didn't want certain things to be published. I have evidence of it. . . . Anne's diary is for me a testament. I must work in her sense. So I decided how to do it through thinking how Anne would have done it. Probably she would have completed it as I did for a publisher." Since the early 1980s, when it became clear that it was *The Diaries of Anne Frank* rather than *The Diary of Anne Frank* that formed the basis for one of the world's best-selling books, people have questioned not only Otto's right to revise his daughter's literary masterpiece but also the extent of his editing. Once asked how much had been omitted, Otto answered, "Nearly nothing has been withheld. A few letters were withheld which deal with personal affairs . . . of people still living. But these don't affect the diary in the least."

Carol Ann Lee, "Ten: Publish Without a Doubt," in *The Hidden Life of Otto Frank*. New York: William Morrow, pp. 214–18, 2003. Copyright © 2003 by Carol Ann Lee. Reprinted by permission of Harper Collins Publishers.

Anne Aspired to Journalism

Anne herself never intended to publish her complete diaries. After hearing [minister for education, art, and science Gerrit] Bolkestein's broadcast, she wrote: "Just imagine how interesting it would be if I were to publish a novel of the *Secret Annex*. The title alone would be enough to make people think it was a detective story." A month later, she declared: "My greatest wish is to become a journalist someday and later on a famous writer. . . . In any case, I want to publish a book entitled *Het Achterhuis* [literally, 'The Behind-House,' i.e., the secret annex] after the war. Whether I shall succeed or not, I cannot say, but my diary will be a great help." By May, she was ready to begin, using sheets of colored carbon paper from the office supplies. She changed words, removed references, added sentences, deleted whole passages, added scenes from memory, and combined entries to make the writing flow. Among the loose pages recently found were two sheets on which Anne had drafted an introduction:

> Writing in a diary is a very new and strange experience for me. I've never done it before, and if I had a close friend I could pour my heart out to, I would never have thought of purchasing a thick, stiff-backed notebook and jotting down all kinds of nonsense that no one will be interested in later on.
>
> But now that I've bought the notebook, I'm going to keep at it and make sure it doesn't get tossed into a forgotten corner a month from now or fall into anyone else's hands. Daddy, Mummy, and Margot may be very kind and I can tell them quite a lot, but my diary and my girlfriend-only secrets are none of their business.
>
> To help me imagine that I have a girlfriend, a real friend who shares my interests and understands my concerns, I won't just write in my diary, but I'll address my letters to this friend-of-my-own-imagination Kitty.
>
> *So here we go!*

Otto chose not to use this introduction.

Anne Revised Her Diary

The fact that both of Anne's versions of the diary were incomplete (her original diary for 1943 was lost, and the second draft finishes four months before they were arrested) presented Otto with a problem. For the period from June 1942 until December 1942, Otto had both diaries from which to work, and usually he stuck to the revised version; for the year 1943 he had only the revised version, and for the period from December 1943 until March 1944 he again had both at his disposal. He had to combine these into one consistent whole. Then he had his own ideas about what was permissible to publish. It is commonly thought that Otto removed the sexual references and those where Anne excessively criticized her mother, but by comparing all three texts we can see that this was not so. It was more often Anne herself who eliminated these details from her revised diary: for instance, her original entry for January 6, 1944, begins with a long passage about her mother, then proceeds to a discussion about sexuality before ending with her decision to make friends with Peter. In her revised diary, Anne completely cut the paragraphs dealing with her mother and sexuality and radically reduces the section concerning Peter. Otto split the long original entry into two ("January 5, 1944," and "January 6, 1944") and kept most of the original version intact. Clearly, Otto was astute enough to realize that part of the diary's power lay in entries such as these, and shrewdly suspecting that they would fascinate the reader, he reinstated them. Despite the various constraints, and with no background in writing or publishing, Otto's editing of his daughter's diary was ingenious.

Otto Reinserted Material

In a private letter, Otto clarified his position: "Anne made an extract of her diaries in which she deleted and changed a great deal of material. . . . But I thought that much of the deleted material was interesting and characteristic . . . so I made a new copy in which I reinserted passages from her diaries." Otto's prologue to the first edition in 1947 read, "With the exception of a few sections, which are meaningless to the reader, the original text has been printed." The first explanation would have made a far more accurate introduction to Anne's legacy. Regardless of this, upon its initial publication, the diary was well received. [The Dutch weekly magazine] *De Groene Amsterdammer* praised "the intelligence, the honesty, the insight with which she observed herself and her surroundings." Asserting that "the talent with which she was able to depict what she saw was astonishing," it declared her "a symbol" of all those murdered in the Holocaust. Other reviews were appreciative but whimsical; *De Vlam*'s [*The Flame*'s] sentiments would be repeated as often as the Westertoren [church bells] chimed in the future: "By no means a war document as such . . . but purely and simply the diary of an adolescent girl."

Anne's Diary Was Well Received

Otto sent copies of the diary to family and friends and to the writers and politicians mentioned in the book. ([Pieter Sjoerds] Gerbrandy, the Dutch prime minister, made a terrible faux pas [social mistake] in addressing his letter of acknowledgment to "Miss Frank.") Otto already felt that the diary could be used in a positive manner; he told Anne's former boyfriend Hello Silberberg that it was "in Anne's spirit that the book should be read as widely as possible, because it should work for people and for humanity. Speak about it, recommend it to others." Laureen Klein, whose wedding to Rudi Nussbaum Otto attended on October 15, 1947, was delighted with the diary's reception: "I read the book as soon as it was published—it really surprised me. I was filled with respect for Anne's literary talent and the way in which she had matured in the intervening years. The fact that she rewrote it with an eye on publication showed that she was destined to be a talented writer. To be honest, I was astounded."

Otto Contracted for Legal Representation

Otto signed a contract with Ernest Kuhn, a New York attorney, who agreed to represent him in negotiations with American and Canadian publishers. Twentieth Century Fox expressed an early interest in the book, but nothing came of it. The diary was in its second printing by the end of the year, and Otto proudly told a relative: "Anne's book is a big success. There have been readings from the book four times already. I hope I can succeed in seeing that English and German editions are also published." [Otto's cousin] Milly [Stanfield] visited Otto in Amsterdam that winter and suspected that publication of the diary had been a significant factor in improving his disposition. She recalled: "The country was certainly at its worst, deep snow everywhere, trams few and far between. But the people were so sturdy and uncomplaining that I found it energizing. Otto showed me all over the annex and introduced me to the wonderful group who, for over two years, had risked their lives daily to help them. . . . The rooms were as Anne described them. Her collection of photos still hung on the walls." The secret annex remained exactly as it had been left on the day of the arrest.

Miep Gies Saved Anne's Diary and Her Legacy

Miep Gies and Alison Leslie Gold

Alison Leslie Gold, known for her writing on Anne Frank and the Holocaust, coauthored Anne Frank Remembered *with Miep Gies. Gold has most recently published* Fiet's Vase and Other Stories of Survival *(2006) and* Lost and Found *which is part of* The Cahier Series *published by the Center for Writers and Translators at the American University of Paris (2010).*

Miep Gies was an office secretary in the business Otto Frank ran before he and his family went into hiding. She was a pivotal player in supporting the family with necessary food, supplies, and news from the outside world, as well as being a guardian of their safety. When the Nazis captured the Franks, Gies gathered up and saved Anne's diary, in spite of the danger of being discovered when the Nazis returned to obliterate the Franks' possessions. Gies, who was born in Austria but relocated to Amsterdam as a young girl, died on January 11, 2010, less than a month before her 101st birthday. She is widely acknowledged as a heroine for saving Anne's diary and her legacy as a writer, but she insisted throughout her life that she did nothing heroic. Gies passed the diary along to Otto Frank when he returned to Amsterdam after the war.

It was just an ordinary Friday morning, August 4, 1944. First thing in the morning, I'd gone into the hiding place to get the shopping list. Lonely after the long night locked in together, my friends were hungry for a good visit. Anne, as usual, had many questions to ask and urged me to talk a little. I promised that I'd come back and sit and we could have a real talk in the afternoon when I returned with the groceries. But conversation would have to wait until then. I went back to the office and got started with my work.

Elli Vossen and Jo Koophuis were working across from me in the office. Sometime between eleven and twelve o'clock, I looked up. There in the doorway stood a man in civilian clothes. I hadn't heard the door. He was holding a revolver, pointing it at us. He came in. "Stay put," he said in Dutch. "Don't move."

Then he walked toward the back office where Mr. Kraler was working, leaving us alone. We were petrified.

Jo Koophuis said to me, "Miep, I think the time has come." . . .

Miep and Her Colleagues Visit the Annex

Then, along the corridor past Mr. Kraler's private office and our office, down the old wooden stairway, I could hear the sound of our friends' feet. I could tell from their footsteps that they were coming down like beaten dogs. . . .

Henk [Gies's husband] said right away to Frits van Matto, "As soon as your assistants have left, lock the door and come back to us." When Van Matto returned, Henk said to Elli, Van Matto, and me, "Now we'll go upstairs and see what the situation is."

Van Matto was carrying the keys that he'd been given. We all went to the bookcase and turned it away from the door leading to the hiding place. The door was locked but otherwise undisturbed. Fortunately, I'd kept a duplicate key, which I went and got. We opened the door and went into the hiding place.

Miep Gies, a Dutch woman who hid Anne Frank from the Nazis and preserved her diary, holds a new translation of The Diary of a Young Girl *published in 1995.* © Associated Press.

Right away, from the door, I saw that the place had been ransacked. Drawers were open, things strewn all over the floor. Everywhere objects were overturned. My eyes took in a scene of terrible pillage.

Miep Finds Anne's Diary

Then I walked into Mr. and Mrs. Frank's bedroom. On the floor, amidst the chaos of papers and books, my eye lit on the little red-orange checkered, cloth-bound diary that Anne had received from her father on her thirteenth birthday. I pointed it out to Elli. Obeying my gesture, she leaned down and picked it up for me, putting it into my hands. I remembered how happy Anne had been to receive this little book to write her private thoughts in. I knew how precious her diary was to Anne. My eyes scanned the rubble for more of Anne's writings, and I saw the old accounting books and many more writing papers that Elli and I had given to her when she had run out of pages in the checkered diary. Elli was still very scared, and looked to me for direction. I told Elli, "Help me pick up all Anne's writings."

Miep Gathers and Hides the Diary

Quickly, we gathered up handfuls of pages in Anne's scrawling handwriting. My heart beat in fear that the Austrian would return and catch us among the now-captured "Jewish possessions." Henk had gathered up books in his arms, including the library books and Dr. Dussel's Spanish books. He was giving me a look to hurry. Van Matto was standing uncomfortably by the doorway. My arms and Elli's arms were filled with papers. Henk started down the stairs. Quickly, Van Matto hurried after him. Elli followed too, looking very young and very scared. I was the last, with the key in my hand.

As I was about to leave, I passed through the bathroom. My eye caught sight of Anne's soft beige combing shawl, with the colored roses and other small figures, hanging on the clothes rack. Even though my arms were filled with papers, I reached out and grabbed the sham with my fingers. I still don't know why.

Trying not to drop anything, I bent to lock the door to the hiding place and returned to the office.

There Elli and I stood facing each other, both loaded down with papers. Elli said to me, "You're older; you must decide what to do."

I opened the bottom drawer of my desk and began to pile in the diary, the old accounting books, and the papers. "Yes," I told Elli, "I will keep everything." I took the papers she was holding and continued filling the drawer. "I'll keep everything safe for Anne until she comes back."

I shut the desk drawer, but I did not lock it. . . .

Miep Is a Safe Haven for the Diary

People in the office asked to see Anne's diary. My answer was always "No. It's not right. Even though it's the writings of a child, it's hers and it's her secret. I'll only return it back into her hands, and her hands alone."

I was haunted by the fact that some more of Anne's pages remained cast around on the floor in the hiding place. I was afraid to go back up there, as [the Austrian, Karl] Silberbauer had already checked on me several times. He'd just pop his head in, saying, "I'm just making sure you haven't gone." I said nothing by way of reply. He'd seen what he wanted, that I hadn't gone anywhere. He'd turn and leave.

I was afraid to go behind the bookcase again. It was very hard for me to look at the rooms with the people gone. I couldn't face going back upstairs.

But I knew that after three or four days Puls movers were going to come to collect the Jewish possessions from the hiding place and ship them to Germany. I said to Van Matto, "Go with the Puls men when they come. Go upstairs and make believe you're helping them clean up. Pick up all the papers like this and bring them to me."

The next day, Puls came. A great truck pulled up in front of our door. I couldn't look as they piled the familiar things, one after another, into the truck. I stayed back from the window, still not believing that it was happening, trying to pretend that our friends were still going about their daily business so close above me.

Van Matto did as I asked, and when they'd left he handed me another pile of Anne's writings. Again, I read nothing, just put the pages together in a neat pile, and added them to the pages already in the bottom drawer of my desk.

Fellow Prisoners at Bergen-Belsen Describe Anne Frank's Last Days

Barry Denenberg

Barry Denenberg was born in 1940 in Brooklyn, New York. He has authored both fiction and historical nonfiction works. He also serves as volunteer director of creative writing and library services at the Waterside School in Stamford, Connecticut, which educates gifted children of low-income families.

While many readers have identified with the Anne Frank of her diary, her eventual fate is not widely known. Denenberg has compiled accounts of Anne's last days in the Bergen-Belsen concentration camp, where she died soon after the death of her sister Margot. These fellow prisoners, who survived the camp, describe the horrific conditions they encountered. They describe how Anne and Margot relied on each other for support and survival. One friend in the camp describes her efforts to supply Anne with food, to little avail. The prisoners believe that Anne lost her will to live when Margot died. The bitter irony is that Anne died one month before Bergen-Belsen was liberated by British soldiers.

At the end of October 1944, the Frank sisters were on a transport headed west, back toward their birthplace, Germany.

> "When our train arrived in Belsen . . . we passed through the barbed-wire gate of the camp without really noticing it, for there was no trace of any camp. No barracks, no crematorium. . . .

Barry Denenberg, "Bergen-Belsen," in *Shadow Life: A Portrait of Anne Frank and Her Family.* New York: Scholastic Press, pp. 177–86, 2005. Reproduced by permission.

There we stood and looked around in astonishment. But soon some curious prisoners came toward us out of the wasteland. Their heads were shaved and they looked in a very bad way.

'Where does one live here?' I asked a woman. 'In tents,' she told me. 'We all sleep on the ground.' 'And is there water here?' 'Not much.' 'Latrines?' 'We have just made a pit for ourselves.' 'And food?' 'Irregular, little of it, and bad.'

We knew what questions to ask when we arrived in a new camp—we had plenty of camp life.... But there was little need to ask many questions. The indications were clear enough."

MRS. RENATE

L.A. [a pseudonym]

Prisoners Used for Slave Labor

Established in 1941 as a prisoner-of-war camp, by 1943 Bergen-Belsen (the names of the two towns it was situated between) had become an "exchange camp." Jewish prisoners with connections abroad, the right papers, or value as hostages were sent there. Eventually they were to be exchanged for German citizens and soldiers being held by the Allies (however, very few ever were). In the meantime they would be used as slave labor for the Third Reich. Families would be allowed to stay together and would remain alive.

Since March 1944, sick and exhausted prisoners—anyone judged unable to work—had been evacuated from other concentration camps and sent to Bergen-Belsen. It was now termed a "recuperation camp" in the ironic, sadistic jargon that hid its true purpose: They had been sent there to die, not recuperate.

The already overcrowded, chaotic camp was unable to properly receive the thousands of people arriving daily. The authorities at Bergen-Belsen hastily constructed tents for temporary housing.

". . . the third night I was there we had a storm. The tents ripped and flew off, and the heavy poles came crashing down on us. The next two nights we slept in a storage shed, among the heaps of SS caps and military boots. On the third day we were driven to a block of barracks that had meanwhile been cleared. That was the beginning of our stay in Belsen."

MRS. RENATE L.A.

Conditions Lead to Illness and Death

The extreme overcrowding and the woeful physical condition of the new arrivals led to hunger, thirst, and rampant disease: dysentery, tuberculosis, and typhus.

There was no water for days at a time, and people died crawling toward the water pump. Some desperately boiled grass, and SS guards were needed when the vat of foul-smelling, barely edible soup was taken to the huts because someone crazed by hunger might attack it. All this occurred while hundreds of Red Cross food parcels containing Ovaltine, canned meat, milk, and biscuits remained unopened and undistributed.

". . . I ran across a woman who I had known at Auschwitz. She had been a block orderly there, and had had decent clothing and food. Now here she stood holding a soup kettle, scraping it out and greedily licking the dregs. When I saw that, I knew enough. It was a bad camp where not even the privileged group had enough to eat. My sister and I looked at one another, and my sister, who had just turned sixteen, said: 'No one will come out of this camp alive.'"

MRS. RENATE L. A.

"The end is the same—only the means are different. In Auschwitz it is a quick, ruthless procedure, mass murder in the gas chambers; in Belsen it is a sadistic, long drawn-out process of starvation, of violence, of terror, of the deliberate spreading of infection and disease."

HANNA LÉVY-HASS

Anne and Margot Struggle to Survive

Anne and Margot clung to each other, trying to survive despite their deteriorating condition and the horror that was enveloping them.

As late fall in northern Germany turned into winter, conditions became even more severe, even more life-threatening. The freezing winds made life that much harder to endure and everyone that much sicker.

Anne and Margot saw a woman they had met at Auschwitz:

> "Anne used to tell stories after we lay down. So did Margot. Silly stories and jokes. We all took our turns telling them. Mostly they were about food. Once we talked about going to the American Hotel in Amsterdam for dinner and Anne suddenly burst into tears at the thought that we would never get back . . . we compiled a menu, masses of wonderful things to eat."
>
> LIENTJE BRILLESLIJPER-JALDATI

> "The Frank girls were almost unrecognizable since their hair had been cut off. They were much balder than we were; how that could be, I don't know. And they were cold, just like the rest of us.

> It was winter and you didn't have any clothes. So all of the ingredients for illness were present. They were in bad shape. Day by day they got weaker. Nevertheless they went to the fence of the so-called free camp every day, in the hopes of getting something. They were very determined. I'm virtually certain that they met someone there whom they knew."
>
> RACHEL VAN AMERONGEN-FRANKFOORDER

Anne's Friend Discovers Her

By the spring of 1944, the overwhelming majority of those living in the so-called Free Camp, a subcamp within Bergen-Belsen, were Dutch. Among them was Lies Goslar, Anne's good friend from Amsterdam.

Lies Goslar's mother had died, along with the baby, giving birth after the Franks went into hiding. In June 1943, Lies, her father, and little sister, Gabi, were rounded up by the Nazis. Because their names were on a list to immigrate to Palestine they were sent from Westerbork to the Free Camp at Bergen-Belsen in February 1944, six months before Anne and the others were discovered in hiding.

In early February 1945, Lies heard that Dutch women from Auschwitz were in the adjacent camp.

"One day a friend of mine tells me, 'You know, between all these women there is your friend Anne Frank.' And I don't know I felt very crazy because I was thinking the whole time Anne is safe and she's in Switzerland. I was sure of this, but this was what [she] said to me and so I had no choice but to go . . . near this barbed wire—this was not allowed. And the German in the watchtower was watching us and you know he would have shot if he would have caught us, but—so we couldn't see . . . there was a barbed wire with straw and we couldn't see the other side. So, I just went near at dark and I would start to call hello, hello? something like this and who answered me but Mrs. van Pals [also spelled 'Pels'].... She said 'You want Anna . . . I will call her for you. Margot I can't call for you, she is very sick already, but Anna I will call for you.'"

HANNELI ELISABETH "LIES" PICK-GOSLAR

Anne's Friend Tries to Provide Food

Auguste van Pels told Lies that Margot was too sick to come but she would get Anne. Separated by the barbed wire the two friends cried; then Anne spoke:

"She said, 'We don't have anything at all to eat here, almost nothing, and we are cold; we don't have any clothes and I've gotten very thin and they shaved my hair.' That was terrible for her. She had always been very proud of her hair. It may have grown back a bit in the meantime, but it certainly wasn't the long hair she'd had before, which she playfully curled around her fingers. . . .

We agreed to meet the next evening at eight o'clock. . . . I succeeded in throwing [a] package [of food] over.

But I heard her screaming, and I called out, 'What happened?'

And Anne answered, 'Oh, the woman standing next to me caught it, and she won't give it back to me.'

Then she began to scream.

I calmed her down a bit and said, 'I'll try again but I don't know if I'll be able to.' We arranged to meet again, two or three days later, and I was actually able to throw over another package. She caught it: That was the main thing.

After these three or four meetings at the barbed-wire fence in Bergen-Belsen, I didn't see her again, because the people in Anne's camp were transferred to another section of Bergen-Belsen. That happened around the end of February. That was the last time I saw Anne alive and spoke to her."

HANNELI ELISABETH "LIES" PICK-GOSLAR

Inhuman Conditions Overpower Anne

Anne was horrified by the lice and had thrown all of her clothes away, even though it was the middle of the winter. She just walked around with a blanket wrapped around her. Both girls had typhus and looked emaciated.

"They were terribly cold. They had the least desirable place in the barracks, below, near the door, which was constantly opened and closed. You heard them constantly screaming, 'Close the door, close the door,' and their voices became weaker every day.

You could really see both of them dying. . . . They were . . . the youngest among us."

RACHEL VAN AMERONGEN-FRANKFOORDER

"It had to have been in March, as the snow was already melting as we went to look for them, but they weren't in the bunk any longer. In the quarantine (sick bunk) is where we found them. We begged them not to stay there, as people in there deteriorated so quickly and couldn't bring themselves to resist, that they'd be soon at the end. Anne simply said, 'Here we both can lie on the plank bed; we'll be together and at peace.' Margot only whispered; she had a high fever.

The following day we went to them again. Margot had fallen from the bed, just barely conscious. Anne also was feverish, yet she was friendly and sweet. 'Margot's going to sleep well, and when she sleeps, I won't have to stay up.'"

LIENTJE BRILLESLIJPER-JALDATI

"Anne was sick, too, but she stayed on her feet until Margot died; only then did she give in to her illness."

JANNY BRANDES-BRILLESLIJPER

Anne, after watching her older sister slowly die, on or near her nineteenth birthday, lost her will to live.

Days later, sometime in late February or early March 1945, Annelies Marie Frank, fifteen, perished, her body thrown in a mass grave.

One month later, on April 15, 1945, Bergen-Belsen was liberated by British soldiers.

Social Issues in Literature

CHAPTER 2

The Diary of a Young Girl and Genocide

Literal and Metaphorical Hiding in *The Diary of a Young Girl*

Karein K. Goertz

Karein K. Goertz is a lecturer in the Residential College of Literature, Science and Arts at the University of Michigan. Her research and teaching include a focus on the Holocaust in literature and film as well as German literature and culture.

In the following selection, Goertz observes that Anne Frank's diary refers to hiding both literally and from Anne's metaphorical perspective as a writer. Goertz states that the Annex is portrayed as both a safe place and an environment where human interaction is magnified, due to the intensity of the ever-present outside menace and the inability to escape the other residents. Anne's hiding, states Goertz, takes the form of writing her innermost thoughts in her diary. Anne hides the true identities of her coresidents with false names. In these ways, Anne creates secret spaces for herself and her family.

The Annex which Anne first describes resonates with [an] archetypal, universal image of the house as shelter and fortress that both protects against and resists the world outside. Otto Frank had spent months transforming the rooms, attic, and loft into a comfortable hiding place. With furniture, decor, and supplies from the family's former life, he sought to preserve the illusion of order, normalcy, and continuity. Anne dedicates many pages of her diary to the description of the Annex as both physical and metaphoric place. When the diary was first published in Holland, it was called *Het Achterhuis*

Karein K. Goertz, "Writing from the Secret Annex: The Case of Anne Frank," *Michigan Quarterly Review*, vol. 39, no. 3, ed. David M. Galens, Jennifer Smith, and Elizabeth Thomason, Summer 2000, pp. 647–59. Copyright © 2000 by Michigan Quarterly Review. Reproduced by permission of the author.

(*The House Behind*) rather than *The Diary of Young Girl*, fore-grounding the spatial over the autobiographical dimension. At first, Anne experiences the Annex in benign terms as part of an adventure or an interlude from reality: "I don't think I'll ever feel at home in this house, but that doesn't mean I hate it. It's more like being on vacation in some strange *pension* [inn]." In her writer's imagination, it gets transformed into a "unique facility for the temporary accommodation of Jews and other dispossessed persons" with strict roles and regulations she describes in a characteristically playful manner: "Diet: low-fat. Free-time activities: None allowed outside the house until further notice." Irony functions as the house does: it is a protective screen that blocks off or hides the anxiety associated with matters of life and death. By choosing to laugh about the absurdity of the situation, she resists its power to defeat her. The Annex is a world away from the world, existing in spite of the world. . . .

The encroaching external menace and constant terror of discovery corrode and suffocate life on the inside. The Annex, once seen as a safe haven, an adventure, a self-contained and sheltering world, is transformed into a prison. She feels like a "songbird whose wings have been ripped off and who keeps hurling itself against the bars of its dark cage." Circumscribed by safety measures, the days follow the same monotonous routine with long hours of oppressive silence and sluggish movement. Anne describes how, after more than a year in hiding, everyone has almost forgotten how to laugh and that she takes daily doses of [the herb] valerian to help combat anxiety and depression.

Anne Retreats into Writing

Anne transforms the privations of everyday life into amusing anecdotes, fear into an interesting adventure story, longing and loneliness into a romance plot. The narratives allow her to distance herself from the situation at hand through irony or retrospective analysis, rather than being submerged by it. They also allow her to explore alternative, more assertive or honest roles she wished she had played. In the claustrophobic context of the Annex, the diary becomes a world into which Anne retreats. Here she can fully express the feelings she must otherwise contain. One can read the diary in spatial terms as a safe place for her real, but still hidden self. It can also be understood in functional terms as a performative sphere in which Anne tests out different versions of herself, giving them a voice and watching them grow. She secures this private domain for herself in direct response to the relentless scrutiny and evaluation of her character by other members in the Annex. These confined quarters where people's moods, thoughts, and fates are so closely intertwined allow very little room for personal unfolding. The diary, like her own person, is under constant threat of being discovered and must therefore be carefully guarded. "Daddy is grumbling again and threatening to take away my diary. Oh horror of horrors! From now on, I'm going to hide it." To assuage the curiosity of the Annex members and to provide them with much-needed comic relief, Anne occasionally reads passages aloud. These readings also serve the purpose of gathering critical feedback on her success as a writer. For the most part, however, Anne considers the diary her own private business and writes under the assumption that it will remain completely confidential. Those from whom she must protect her diary are not the Annex members alone, but also the outside world. Two months after arriving in the Annex, Anne rereads her first diary entries about this initially "ideal place" and adds that she is terrified that the hiding place will be revealed and its inhabitants shot. This fear explains why she omits the name of the man who supplies the Annex with potatoes. She knows that, if discovered, the diary could potentially be used as incriminating evidence against their helpers. Later, when she begins revising her diary for a future audience, she uses pseudonyms to protect the real identities of the Annex members. This coded language reveals yet another level of hiding. . . .

Voices of Others Are Hidden

Inevitably, people and events described in a diary are introduced to us through the biased perspective of the writer. From reported speech and described actions, we may be able to glean the personalities and motivations of secondary characters, but our understanding of them within the context of the diary is always limited and shaped by the narrator. In her diary, Anne describes the most intimate details of the other seven members of the Annex, yet we never come to know them as complex individuals. At times, they seem to be mere caricatures of qualities Anne either emulates or despises: Margot, ever-patient and selfless; Otto, compassionate and understanding; Mrs. van Daan, nosy and bossy. Recent biographies and documentaries have sought to give a voice to—and bring out of hiding—those Annex members who suffered the "fury of her pen." Edith Frank, whom Anne at one point angrily disavows as her mother, and the middle-aged dentist Fritz Pfeffer, whom Anne nicknamed Dussel (dope), bear the brunt of her criticism. Of the latter, we only see the "old-fashioned disciplinarian and preacher of unbearably long sermons on manners." We never get to know the man who sent clandestine love letters to a woman he was forced to leave because racial laws made it illegal for them to marry. Nor do we learn that he had a son, approximately Anne's age, whom he had put on a children's transport train to London in 1938 so that he would survive the war in safety with an uncle. In Jon Blair's documentary film *Anne Frank Remembered* (1995), Pfeffer's son conveys the bitter imprint Anne's diary has left on his life. Whereas Otto Frank became an icon of the perfect, caring father for generations of young girls, his father, with whom he had lost contact after the outbreak of the war, was harshly and unfairly portrayed. As Melissa Müller reveals in *Anne Frank:*

The Biography, the recently recovered pages present a fuller picture of Anne's relationship toward her mother. In the pages Otto Frank removed because he felt the public did not need to know about his marriage, Anne expresses sympathy and understanding for her mother whose passion for her husband was not reciprocated. Without this piece of information that explains why Edith Frank may have become "somewhat defensive and unapproachable," we see her only as a source of deep disappointment and frustration for her daughter

The Voice of All Jewish Children

Not only does the diary contain silenced or hidden voices within it, one can also observe how for many years Anne Frank stood in for all children during the Holocaust. Generally speaking, scholarship did not begin to focus on the fate of children until forty years after the war, even though being a Jewish child in Europe meant certain extermination. Only 6–7% of Jewish children survived the Holocaust, compared with a 33% survival rate among adults. Most of these children survived the war in hiding. Some remained "visible," passing as Christians in convents, monasteries, orphanages, or with foster families. They were forced to live double lives with new names and assumed identities. Survival depended upon concealing their emotions, remaining silent, and playing roles. Others remained "invisible" for months, even years, hiding out in attics, woods, barns, and other makeshift places, constantly vulnerable to discovery. Many lost not only their childhood, but also their identity, their families, and their lives. The prolonged public silence about hidden children may have to do with a general inability or reluctance to reconcile ideas of childhood with war. As countries grappled first with the shocking revelations of the death camps in the immediate postwar period and then tried to put the past behind them in the years of reconstruction, no room was given to the fate of children in public discourse. Anne Frank's story—that is, the one that ends *before* her deportation to and death in Bergen-Belsen—was the exception. . . .

Readers Identify with Anne

Identification with Anne's story has been particularly strong among adolescent girls who feel alienated from their parents while observing their own rapid internal changes with bewilderment and fascination. The diary mirrors their struggle for independence and search for a genuine voice. For adults, Anne is frequently seen as a universalized victim and "symbol of the oppressed." Her diary stands in defiance of injustice and serves as a "testament to courage, hope, and the faith in human goodness." In some political situations, Anne has functioned as a role model. [Former political prisoner and later president of South Africa] Nelson Mandela describes how the diary was smuggled into South African prisons during the years of apartheid, giving inmates the will to endure their suffering. Anne has also been an inspiration for writers who recognize and admire in her their own nascent desire to write. These multiple points of identification explain the ongoing, deep impact of the diary, but can also be problematic. Reading the diary as a classic portrait of adolescence, for example, glosses over the anxieties and all-too-real dangers associated with the particular historical context of the Holocaust. Early Broadway and Hollywood adaptations of the diary demonstrate how Anne's story was transformed into an "infantilized, Americanized, homogenized and sentimentalized" story of general human interest that had little, if anything, to do with Jewish suffering. . . .

Understanding the Impact of Hiding

Next to exile, hiding was one of the few alternatives Jews had to escape or postpone death. Examining this most extreme, literal form of hiding in conjunction with its other, more metaphoric meanings yields a nuanced understanding of the external and internal conditions that created the diary. With the inclusion of five new pages into future editions of the diary, yet another part of Anne Frank's emotional and fantasy life will have been brought out of hiding into the public sphere. With them, the once intimate hideaway will be fully exposed. Just as the diary and its reception reveal different levels of hiding and uncovering, it has, for better or for worse, invited many kinds of identifications and appropriations. The blank page that follows the final signature "Yours, Anne M. Frank" has been and will continue to be an invitation for writers to fill. Their responses may open up new questions and readings between the lines of the diary. It is this multilayered quality that lies at the heart of the diary's success both as historical testimony and as literature.

Anne Frank's Diary Brought Awareness to Women's and Children's Holocaust Experiences

Martha Ravits

Martha Ravits was a university professor for twenty years and has published numerous academic articles, with an emphasis on women in literature and on Jewish literature.

In the article that follows, Ravits asserts that the debut of Anne Frank's diary in the English-speaking world brought women's and children's experiences during the Holocaust to the forefront of literature. Anne's writing gave form to the anonymity of millions who were murdered by the Nazis. In the conformity-ridden culture of the 1950s, which included a strong strain of anti-Semitism, according to Ravits, the diary gave American Jews a nonthreatening vehicle to appeal to the conscience of the public. The diary also served to reinforce the importance of women's writing about the Holocaust and the legitimacy of the diary as an art form.

Often women's history and literature need to be recovered from the past, salvaged from obscurity, but the public reception of Anne Frank's diary helped ensure that women's and children's experiences were never excluded from the Holocaust as a field of study. Rather, from its inception, men, women's, and children's stories were regarded as crucial elements in understanding [Nazi leader Adolf] Hitler's war against the Jews. Elie Wiesel [a novelist who survived the Holocaust] claims that as "the Greeks invented tragedy, the Romans the epistle

Martha Ravits, "To Work in the World: Anne Frank and American Literary History," *Women's Studies*, vol. 27, no. 1, 1997, pp. 1, 78–81. Reproduced by permission.

and the Renaissance the sonnet, our generation invented a new literature, that of testimony." The category of postwar literature that Wiesel describes has grown so tremendously and come to seem so self-evident in our culture that its American origins tend to be forgotten. Even at the distance of a mere half century, remembering how we began the vast and difficult project of remembering the Holocaust requires some reconstruction. For after the devastation of World War II, there was a delay—a dropped stitch in the fabric of historical time—before the general population received and absorbed the news of genocide in Europe. . . .

An Introduction to Holocaust Literature

Anne Frank's debut in this country, seven years after the end of the war, in a sense marks the debut of Holocaust literature. Although the Holocaust has since altered the moral dimensions of twentieth-century thought and literature, in 1952 the Nazi atrocities were not generally understood to have been directed against the Jews (along with others, such as Gypsies and homosexuals). America awaited a major event to galvanize public opinion about genocide during a period marked by "numbness," "denial," and "repression" of the massive suffering in Europe. Under such circumstances, preparations for publishing testimony by a Jewish victim inaugurated intense debate over how to present the material most effectively for popular consumption—as a work of universal pathos or as a work of ethnic specificity.

During the economic prosperity of the [President Dwight D.] Eisenhower years, the American Jewish minority made visible strides in social and economic standing. Assimilation into mainstream life held out the promise of further advances (perhaps easing of the quota system), just when American Jews were dealt a staggering blow by revelations coming out of postwar Europe about the Final Solution [the Nazi plan for systematic genocide]. Added to this assault was information about the refusal of the U.S. government to rescue European Jewish refugees during the crisis. The anti-Semitism unleashed in Europe loomed as a horrifying specter with implications for Jews everywhere. Thus, American Jews felt keenly sensitive about how the story of the Holocaust should be related to the Christian society at large. Some Jews wanted to protest loudly against ethnic atrocities; others were wary about arousing latent anti-Semitism at home by appearing to confirm the stereotype of the pushy or aggressive Jew. The diary of a young female victim seemed an ideal vehicle for surmounting these obstacles and appealing to the nation's conscience. As an assimilated Western European Jew, Anne Frank was easily reassimilated to American standards. Her book was, after all, a captivity narrative complete with brave Christian protectors, youthful ambitions for self-betterment, and first love—all themes that corresponded well to American ideals and the temper of the times.

Refined for Popular Consumption

The diary had originally been published in Holland in 1947 under the title Anne Frank herself had chosen, *Het Achterhuis [The House Behind]*. Five years later when it was translated for publication in America, the title was changed to *The Diary of a Young Girl*, a shift in wording intended to promote the work as that of an innocent child distanced from the sphere of adult ideology, though that was not how Frank saw herself: "I know what I want, I have a goal, have an opinion, have a religion and love. Let me be myself and then I am satisfied. I know that I'm a woman, a woman with inward strength and plenty of courage!" (9 April, 1944). The socio-political climate in the United States at the time of the diary's release—a time of recuperation, materialism, and dull conformity—militated against allowing her simply to be herself. Anne Frank's reflections on anti-Semitism and on "the woman question" were toned down or even omitted when the diary was transformed for the popular media. The title was just the first in a series of refinements meant to present Anne Frank as an innocent and idealistic female—not a speculative young thinker who explored mature and controversial issues in her writings.

In addition to ideological compatibility, sheer timing—priority of place—contributed to Anne Frank's success in America. It was not that she was alone but that she alone was so effective in arousing a sense of identification and sympathy about what had previously been reams of dire statistics and dehumanizing photographs in a country separated both geographically and psychologically from the decimation in Europe. Collections of Holocaust eye-witness accounts and documentation had previously been assembled, but they had not resounded much beyond Jewish and intellectual circles. . . .

The diary that launched this cycle of increasing public awareness first arrived in America as a slim daybook by an unknown Jewish teenager. After the war, when American-Jewish writer Meyer Levin was in Europe to cover the story of the concentration camps, he was given a French copy of Anne Frank's diary by his wife. In its pages, he believed he had discovered a voice from among the countless victims of Hitler that could awaken the conscience of the world. He immediately wrote to Otto Frank offering assistance in finding an American publisher for the diary. Levin recounts his involvement with the project in his aptly titled memoir, *The Obsession.* . . .

Importance of the Woman's Perspective

The diary was a breakthrough on several fronts. Because Anne Frank delineates moral imperatives from the perspective of a Holocaust victim and a woman, the diary crosses categories of history and literature, private and public writing, gender and genre. The unprecedented success of *The Diary of a Young Girl* proved that an adolescent and a woman—someone twice removed from the established circles of literary authority—

Holocaust survivor Berthe Badehi visits an exhibit at Jerusalem's Yad Vashem Museum about the Nazi treatment of women. The Diary of a Young Girl *is credited with bringing awareness to the plight of women and children during the Holocaust.* © Reuters/Yonathan Weitzman.

could leave an imprint on the world of literature and ideas. A decade before the social crusade of the women's movement and nearly two decades before feminist scholars within the academy began to press for inclusion of women's works in the predominantly male canon, *The Diary of a Young Girl* proved the importance of women's writing that lay outside the purview of traditional literary boundaries, just as the perverse polymorphism of women's writing would challenge established literary concepts in the decades ahead. And the overwhelming popularity of the diary meant that for the first time in this century the work of a woman became the standard against which all subsequent literature in a given field was to be measured. Critics and reviewers in every decade since its publication have invoked the name of Anne Frank in evaluating personal accounts of war or social upheaval. . . .

On March 28, 1944, Anne Frank and the others in the attic gathered round their forbidden radio and heard a London broadcast by the Dutch government in exile in which Gerrit Bolkestein, Minister of Art and Education, stressed the need to publish memoirs by ordinary citizens after the war—he mentioned letters and diaries specifically—to record for posterity the sufferings of the Dutch people under German occupation. Anne Frank grasped a way to publish her diary and started to work on revisions—refining and enlarging the original draft. She even prepared a list of pseudonyms to shield the identities of the people described in her pages. "My greatest wish," she wrote, "is to become a journalist someday and later on a famous writer. Whether these leanings towards greatness (insanity!) will ever materialize remains to be seen. . . . I want to publish a book entitled Het Achterhuis after the war" (11 May, 1944). By the end of the period in hiding she thought of herself as a writer and was revising the diary at the pace of as many as ten pages a day.

The Writer's Mode of Survival

Her art reaches fever pitch in the closing months of the diary, as the bombings over Amsterdam intensified and she worked with increasing talent in what proved to be a futile race against time. Once, when depressed, she made a chilling prediction (in hindsight an eerie, hypothetical reversal of fate): "I have now reached the stage that I don't care much whether I live or die. The world will keep on turning without me . . . but should I be saved, and spared from destruction, then it would be terrible if my diaries and my tales were lost" (3 February, 1944). The diary reveals a dedicated writer who was clear-sighted about moods of self-confidence and self-doubt. By highlighting her optimism and evading her bouts of depression, the American popularizers in the 1950s distort the record. She battled insomnia, depression, hunger, and eye strain, pouring her physical strength into the labor of writing. In passages, she carefully revisited and reweighed her reasons for optimism, a sign of her growing apprehension that "hope" is a writer's imaginative construct, an enabling strategy for psychic and artistic survival. . . .

No text can escape ideology, but recent editions of the diary of Anne Frank make it possible to reappraise the full scope of her opinions against the overlay of 1950s ideology that helped shape her fame in America. The popular media stressed Frank's youth and idealism in efforts to transcend barriers of ethnic difference; the fact that she was female made those modifications easier. But readers of the diary (as opposed to viewers of the play or film) find more substantive complexity. In the annals of American literature Anne Frank plays a dualistic role. She wears the mantle of the 1950s anointed "young girl," the media darling, and the cloak of the female writer, posing existential questions, chafing at gender constraints, living in dread of death, but nonetheless writing and revising up to the end. "My feeling for justice is immovable," she wrote on 9 April, 1944, a few months before her arrest and deportation. Proud inheritor of a German-Jewish ethical tradition that abhors injustice and exalts human rights, she added women rights to that list and inscribed it into the annals of postwar literature as a living legacy.

Wiesel's *Night* and Frank's Diary Reflect Different Perspectives on Genocide

Mary D. Lagerwey

Mary D. Lagerwey is a professor in the Bronson School of Nursing at Western Michigan University. She has written extensively for numerous professional and educational publications about gender issues and the values and related ethical issues of nursing, especially during wartime and in the context of religion.

While both Elie Wiesel and Anne Frank wrote about their experience as adolescents during the Holocaust, Frank's account ends when her family is taken away by the Nazis. Wiesel's story, written as an adult, is the linchpin in a lifetime of writing and recognition. In this selection, Lagerwey postulates that Wiesel's story resonates as part of the grand male narrative of struggle and survival, written by an adult male. In contrast, Frank's story has become the story for all Jews who were murdered in the Holocaust. Further, states Lagerwey, Frank wrote as an adolescent girl who speaks with less authority than a grown man, and her diary was edited after her death to make it more palatable to a general readership.

*N*ight and *Anne Frank: The Diary of a Young Girl* have received extensive academic and public attention in the United States. Two clear patterns emerge. First, Anne Frank, author of one major work is syntactically and conceptually inseparable from her diary. All references to her include references to her diary. Furthermore, recent edition of other writings of hers, such as her short stories collected as *Anne Frank's*

Mary D. Lagerwey, "Reading Anne Frank and Elie Wiesel: Voice and Gender in Stories of the Holocaust," *Contemporary Jewry*, vol. 17, 1996, pp. 49–58. Copyright © 1996 by Springer Science + Business Media. Reproduced by permission of the publisher and the author.

Tales from the Secret Annex, include prominent references to her diary. In contrast, as a survivor, Elie Wiesel has received much media attention apart from his memoir, and has written numerous scholarly and popular articles and books. His fame extends to his political activities, and his role as a "messenger" from the Holocaust. References to Elie Wiesel outnumber specific references to *Night* by over ten to one.

Different Adolescent Perspectives

Second, although each tells a story of adolescence during the Holocaust, Anne Frank wrote as an adolescent and Elie Wiesel wrote as an adult, about an adolescent. The attention paid to *Night* follows more closely traditional indicators of canonical status, with prominence in [Modern Language Association] listings, and rare notation as juvenile literature. Anne Frank's diary shows more public attention, reflecting its unique immediacy for young readers, and its use as an introduction to the Holocaust for secondary school readers. Her diary is, therefore, more likely to be classified as juvenile literature. This is most clearly demonstrated in the *Biography Index*, in museum bibliographies and the [American Sociological Association's] near-omission of Anne Frank's work in college-level syllabi. As [Holocaust historian Deborah] Lipstadt describes the diary, "for many readers it is their introduction to the Holocaust."

Yet, Anne Frank's and Elie Wiesel's stories have certain parallels. They were born only one year apart, Frank in 1929 and Wiesel in 1928. In 1944, each was sent by train with their families to Auschwitz. Each survived initial selections there, and lived for some months with a same-sex parent. Neither of these parents survived the war. Each was taken from Auschwitz before liberation: Frank to Bergen-Belsen, and Wiesel to Buchenwald. Miraculously, some of each of their immediate families survived: Frank's father and Wiesel's sisters.

There are, however, important differences: most notably, Frank died shortly before liberation, while Wiesel survived. Frank's work was published first in Dutch in 1947, and in English in 1952. It preceded Wiesel's original Yiddish 1956 memoir by nine years, and the 1960 English publication of *Night* by eight.

The Diary as Coming-of-Age Story

Anne Frank's voice was heard as far back as the early 1950s and resonates through the decades. For many young girls in the United States in the 1950s and 1960s, her voice was not only a voice from the Holocaust, but a solitary voice speaking for us in a frightening world in which our female stories were silenced or unspoken. According to [author and English professor emerita Phyllis] Rose,

> Anne Frank stood for all the Jews who were murdered in the Holocaust. [Yet,] she also stood for adolescent girls trying to assert their individuality in the complicated context of family life. . . . Anne Frank had a special meaning to girls. For she was real, not a fictional creation. And she had written herself into being.

In this reading, Frank represents not only Holocaust victims, but a young girl coming of age. . . .

Wiesel's Story Is of a Survivor

Elie Wiesel provides another prominent voice from the Holocaust speaking through the years for Holocaust survivors. Born just one year before Anne Frank, he tells an alternative story, although contemporaneous with hers. For many, Wiesel's story, powerfully told, darkly written, has become *the* story of an Auschwitz survivor, if not *the* story of a Holocaust survivor. His book, *Night*, was the first well-known memoir of a Holocaust survivor. He serves on Presidential Commissions, appears on late-night television and writes the foreword for the *Encyclopedia of the Holocaust*.

Elie Wiesel, a Romanian-born Holocaust survivor, accepts the Nobel Peace Prize on December 19, 1986. His best-selling memoir Night *is considered an important contribution to Holocaust literature on par with Anne Frank's* The Diary of a Young Girl. © Associated Press.

In 1956, long before he was well-known, Wiesel first published his memoir *Night* in Yiddish under the title, *The World Was Silent*. In 1958 an abridged version was translated into French. And in 1960, the French version was translated into

English in the United States and given the current title, *Night*. In 1996 he published his memoirs, the story of his life from childhood to the present. While Wiesel's early works were not widely reviewed at the time of publication, *Night* is now almost uniformly included in bibliographies and syllabi on the Holocaust. It has been translated into over 18 languages. . . .

The Male's Grand Narrative

Wiesel's words capture much of the horror for the Jewish community, from ghetto to trains to camp, through selections, death, and—for a remnant—liberation. His story contains the major elements of the (male) Auschwitz grand narrative. . . .

It is no accident that the representative story of a Holocaust survivor is of an adult male, and the representative story of a victim is of a young female. I, too, initially thought of them as a child and an adult, and referred to them as "Anne" and "Wiesel." I then purposefully replaced these with full names. While Elie Wiesel speaks for survivors, Anne Frank speaks for those killed in the camps. Her voice, [Meyer] Levin asserts, "becomes the voice of six million vanished Jewish souls." She remains in our thoughts forever young, forever fifteen. Anne Frank speaks for the dead, for children, and thus tells us a story not of an exemplary life, but of a sympathetic victim.

Frank's and Wiesel's stories follow many conventions of Western writing. Wiesel, an adult male, represents for many in the United States all Holocaust survivors. His voice speaks with coherence. It has come into prominence following international recognition of him as a representative "successful" Holocaust survivor. He, unlike Frank, is truly the author of all stages of his work: initial writing, editing, rewriting, and answering challenges to the veracity of his words. . . .

Gender Differences in Style

Many well-known stories of the Holocaust speak to us through the voices of men, voices mistakenly taken to speak for all those who experienced the Holocaust. [According to Holocaust scholar Myrna Goldenberg]:

> English language audiences know Holocaust literature primarily through male writers and have generalized those experiences to represent the whole.... Narratives by women survivors, however, form a group that differs significantly from those by men.

Except for Anne Frank's story, texts of Holocaust memories have been primarily male. As ... Holocaust scholar [Marlene E. Heinemann] notes:

> The study of Holocaust literature has focussed primarily on the writings of men, whose perspectives have been taken as representative of the experience of all Holocaust victims.... However, research which implies "universality" through men's writing and experience is inadequate.

Autobiography theory and research consistently point to patterns of gendered differences in self-writing. Moreover, these patterns are not only evident in the form and reception of the *Diary*, but may be largely responsible for its renown. The genre of Anne Frank's work, a semi-private diary, and her victim status have constituted its appeal for over half a century. Frank began her diary on June 12, 1942, addressing an imaginary friend, "I hope I will be able to confide everything to you, as I have never been able to confide in anyone, and I hope you will be a great source of comfort and support." Frank here follows the conventions of diary as a private "record of (secret) truth," [in the words of authors Wendy J. Wiener and George C. Rosenwald]....

Not the Only Author of Her Story

In contrast to Elie Wiesel, Anne Frank has not been the sole author of her work. The histories of her story—publication, production and controversy—point to her posthumous fame, but also to the lack of power, control and authority she has had over the fate of her story. Her words have been edited by others: her father edited the original published work, and each translation has edited and rewritten her words to make them palatable and acceptable to the general public. Each translation has conceded "alterations and suppression of material from the original diary," [according to Jewish studies professor and author Alvin Rosenfeld].

Anne Frank does not author the ending of her own story. Her story does not end with her words. Instead, it has many endings, all written by others. [Writer and documentarian Ernst] Schnabel edited a collection of stories about Anne Frank, told by forty-two people who had known her. Thirty years later, six women who had known Anne Frank during the months between her last diary entry and her death told her stories through a Dutch television film documentary and a collection of their tales, *The Last Seven Months of Anne Frank*, now available in English. . . .

A Child Forever

Anne Frank's story and her life are objects manipulated (perhaps for gain) by others. She is outside the realm of adult issues of power and control, and remains forever a child. Her writing conforms to the genres common to women's self-writing: letters, diaries and private journals. Ironically, while women speak frequently in genres of self-writing, and critics traditionally decode their texts as autobiographical, the genre of autobiography has been privileged male writing. . . .

Part of the appeal of Anne Frank's story is the ease with which it remains simultaneously exemplary and "other," representative and marginal. Her voice, though prominent and renowned, is nonetheless comfortably the voice of a child and therefore speaks with little authority. Anne Frank remains "other" at many levels: as female, Jew, Holocaust victim and child. Her diary, not corresponding to the literary convention of autobiography as the story of a great man, has achieved academic attention primarily in response to challenges to its authenticity.

Anne Frank's Diary Sentimentalizes Genocide

Judith Goldstein

Judith Goldstein is the founder and executive director of Humanity in Action, an organization that sponsors fellowships for college students and recent graduates in the United States and Europe. Humanity in Action develops a network of young people and existing leaders with a commitment to protecting minorities and promoting human rights in their own communities and around the world.

In the essay that follows, Goldstein asserts that the sense of optimism and faith in people with which Anne Frank's diary has been imbued is misplaced. Frank's story has been elevated to that of a myth, while overlooking the real terror and fear of her life in the Annex. Christianity has applied its own template to Frank, states Goldstein, and reinterpreted her life as one of a saint. Further, the Dutch culture included a paradoxical view and treatment of the Jews in their midst. Over time, Dutch Jews disappeared from daily life, as they fled the country, went into hiding, or were captured by the Nazis. Goldstein says that the Dutch portrayed ambivalent views about the Jews who returned to the Netherlands after the war.

For millions of people, Anne Frank's history has come to symbolize one of Europe's deadliest conflagrations—a time when one nation set fire to its democratic government, ravaged countries all over the continent, destroyed Jewish life in Eastern Europe, and irreparably damaged Jewish existence in many Western European countries, as well. . . .

An aura of sweet optimism and faith surrounds the Diary. Unfortunately, the sentiments are misapplied. [Essayist] Cyn-

Judith Goldstein, "Anne Frank: The Redemptive Myth," *Partisan Review*, vol. 70, no. 1, Winter 2003, p. 16. Copyright © 2003 by Partisan Review. Reproduced by permission of the author.

thia Ozick's is closer to the truth. She described the Diary as a "chronicle of trepidation, turmoil, alarm. . . . Betrayal and arrest always threaten. Anxiety and immobility rule. It is a story of fear." People know that Anne, her sister, and her mother were exterminated, but for many readers Anne's story ends with the hope that "people are really good at heart." These words, I believe, are the key to understanding the conversion of her diary and persona into a redemptive myth.

Anne Frank Has Been Sanctified

[Journalist and historian] Ian Buruma wrote that Anne Frank has "become a Jewish Saint Ursula, a Dutch Joan of Arc, a female Christ." He concluded, "Anne is a ready-made icon for those who have turned the Holocaust into a kind of secular religion." I would take the comparisons even further. Despite the evolution of Europe's postwar secular spirit, the myth derives much of its force from a deeply ingrained Christian template. Anne's story converges on elements of Christian belief and symbolism: a hidden child, a virgin, a betrayal, the Holocaust as Hell, a form of resurrection through words. The redemptive tale seems tragically simple, but the real history is complex and convoluted. It is part of a national tragedy in a country of contradictions. The German occupation exacerbated passive political and social habits that affected the individual and collective life of the Dutch. The Anne Frank legend has further blurred the history of Dutch Jews and the Dutch nation during the War. A sorting out is long overdue.

The Dutch Culture Accepted the Jews

In an essay published in early 1981, the American historian Simon Schama highlighted some of those Dutch paradoxes in regard to the Jews. Schama was writing about [Dutch painter] Rembrandt's time, when Jews were welcomed in Amsterdam but also subject to restrictions in terms of occupation, membership in guilds, political rights, and religious expression. In his introduction to an exhibition of Rembrandt's images of Jews in the Netherlands, Schama wrote, "The relationship of the host culture to its Jewish immigrants was . . . clouded with ambiguities." He continued, "Compared with other seventeenth century options, it cannot be overstressed, the Dutch Republic was a paradise of toleration and security." He described Amsterdam in the seventeenth century as a "relatively benevolent milieu" for Jews—one in which they could develop an identity in the Dutch context. . . .

The Jewish population in the Netherlands continued to expand and confidently regarded itself as part of the Dutch nation. In Rembrandt's time, the Jewish population was 10,000. Two centuries later, it was 140,000. By 1940, many Jews had attained high levels of prosperity, recognition, and acceptance in Dutch life, although not to the degree characteristic of German Jews before the rise of [German leader Adolf] Hitler. Forty percent of the Jewish population lived in small villages, towns, or cities such as the Hague. The other 60 percent lived in Amsterdam. A large number of them were poor. Through the 1930s, Dutch Jews focused on internal issues of assimilation, integration, and the well-being of the Jewish community despite the fact that Nazi rule in Germany compelled thousands of Jews, such as Otto Frank, to seek refuge in the Netherlands.

Jews Were Segregated When Germany Conquered the Netherlands

The Dutch haven appeared secure until the spring of 1940, when Germany conquered the Netherlands. The Dutch fought for five days and then capitulated. . . .

It didn't take long for the Germans to differentiate Jews from other Dutch citizens through anti-Jewish decrees and administrative acts: first, prohibition against Jewish civil servants and teachers; then, in 1941, violent assaults against Jews in the Jewish Quarter in Amsterdam. . . .

Initially, German policies of disenfranchisement and persecution infuriated the Dutch. In February 1941, they launched a general strike, which closed down the docks, the transportation system, and industry. This great spasm of opposition to the Germans—and outrage against the treatment of the Jews—lasted three days. The punitive German response pushed the Dutch back into acquiescence and did nothing to stop the increasing physical isolation of the Jews, their economic ruination, and the eventual roundups and deportations. Resistance flared again in the spring of 1942, when every Dutch Jew was ordered to buy and wear a yellow star with "Jew" written on it. Many Dutch non-Jews wore the yellow star or a yellow flower in solidarity. It made a strong impression on Miep Gies, protector of the Frank family. "The yellow stars and yellow flowers those first few days were so common," she wrote in her book *Anne Frank Remembered*, "that our River Quarter was known as the Milky Way. . . . A surge of pride and solidarity swelled briefly until the Germans started cracking heads and making arrests. A threat was delivered to the population at large: anyone assisting Jews in any way would be sent to prison and possibly executed."

Many Dutch Jews Hid or Fled

Life for Jews in the Netherlands ground down to a devastating pattern of anxiety and violent roundups for Jews, their protectors, and those in the resistance movement. Unlike the Jews in Denmark who could escape to Sweden, the Dutch Jews had nowhere to go. Some, such as the Franks, withdrew into hiding. They were totally dependent on their Dutch protectors who resisted the Germans by housing, feeding, clothing, and caring for Jews. Of the 140,000 Jews in the Netherlands in 1940, about 20,000 went into hiding. Approximately 7,000 of them were discovered. They shared the fate of the majority of Dutch Jews: removal to the Westerbork camp and then deportation to Sobibor and Auschwitz in the East. By the time the process was complete, 110,000 Dutch Jews had been killed.

Jews Disappeared from Daily Life in the Netherlands

The German occupation sorely challenged traditional Dutch attitudes, built upon a seemingly strong facade of tolerance and compromise. The political and social acceptance of differences obscured the fateful gulf between tolerance, on the one hand, and disinterest and disengagement, on the other. In regard to national cohesion and separate ethnic, religious, and political identities, the war tested the viability of the so-called Dutch pillar society, based upon separate realms of allegiance among Protestant, Catholic, Socialist, and Liberal groups. With insidious understanding of these affiliations and, above all else, the Dutch yearning for order, the Germans surgically removed the Jews from Dutch life. And so the Jews disappeared from the realm of moral concern.

Despite the humiliation and anxiety of occupation, only in the last year of the war did the non-Jewish Dutch—principally those in the large northern cities—suffer acutely from the depletion of goods and dangers of forced labor in Germany. The German defeat finally came to the northern part of the country on May 4, 1945. When the Germans finally surrendered, the Dutch celebrated in the streets for days. The Queen returned. "People who had been in hiding came out onto the streets," Miep Gies wrote. "Jews came out of hiding places, rubbing eyes that were unused to sunlight, their faces yellow and pinched and distrustful. Church bells rang everywhere; streamers flew. . . . To wake up and go through a whole day without any sense of danger was amazing." . . .

Returning Jews Were Expected to Make Do

[Miep Gies's] friends included nine Jews who had been hiding above the offices where Gies had worked for Otto Frank's firm. Day after day she asked returning Jews if they had seen any of the Frank family. In June, Otto Frank returned to the Netherlands from Auschwitz with the news that his wife had died there. He was unsure about what had happened to his two children, Margot and Anne. Months later he got word from a nurse in Rotterdam that the daughters had not survived their imprisonment in Auschwitz and Bergen-Belsen. The finality of all the deaths mixed into the tortured lives of those who survived. "I heard it said," Gies wrote in her book, "that where the Jews had looked like everyone else before [the war], after what they had endured, those who returned looked different. But people hardly noticed because everyone had been through so much misery that no one had much interest in the suffering of others." Despite the fact that Dutch Jewry lost nearly 75 percent of its population—the highest number of deaths in any Western European country under occupation—despite the fact that the Dutch Jews had lost everything, the few who came back were expected to make do with what they found, or did not find, of their former lives. . . .

The survivors were told to be quiet—to keep their nightmares and losses to themselves. A once thriving Jewish Dutch world of family, community, institutions, and property was gone. The Dutch constructed effective bureaucratic remedies to bury Jewish claims to emotional and full financial restitution. Many survivors retreated into silence as European countries began to rebuild, to cleanse themselves, and to adjust to the development of the Iron Curtain.

The Dutch Constructed Myths About Their Nazi Resistance

Amidst rebuilding civilized life in the postwar world, Europeans and Americans constructed comforting wartime myths, especially myths about resistance. This is particularly true about the Dutch, who sought to restore a viable nation after the trauma of occupation and the erosion of the pillar society.

In a seminal essay, [researchers] Matthijs Kronemeijer and Darren Teshima described this process:

> [This new] identity was built upon the heroic stories of re-sistance in the Netherlands to the Nazi regime and the belief that Dutch society had stood by and protected its Jewish citizens. While individual acts of heroism and resistance cer-tainly existed, the formation of a national myth focused on these acts and extending this heroism to describe the entire Dutch nation obfuscated the truth of the war experience.

The world thinks that the Franks were emblematic of what happened to the Jews in the Netherlands. From Anne's story, the international public has gained the impression that whole Jewish families could go into hiding together; that most could remain in one place for a few years; that numerous Christian friends or employees could sustain and succor them in hiding; and that the unfortunate hidden Jews were the ones betrayed by some unknown informer. And there was the final impres-sion: that after the war Dutch Jews would be welcomed back to the country in which they had lived.

In the Netherlands, as in all European countries, there were extremes of valor and decency along with villainy, greed, brutality, and cowardice. In the large middle ground there were bystanders who lived with fear and indifference to the threatened minority. . . .

The history of Otto Frank and his family was unique in many ways. Most of the Dutch were too afraid of German ter-ror and punishment to aid those in hiding and most couldn't be sure that their neighbors could be trusted. Most Jewish families were broken up, as children were sent away by them-selves into hiding and people had to move from place to place to escape detection. Many Amsterdam Jewish families were too poor to pay for places to hide, although a considerable number of Dutch protected Jews without initially asking for payment. And then, after the war, most Dutch Jews came back to a society that was largely indifferent or cruelly hostile to what the Jews had suffered. Otto Frank's welcome was an exception. Miep Gies and her husband, who had protected and aided the Franks in hiding, received him warmly, brought him into their family for seven years, and helped him to rebuild his life.

Anne Frank's Annex Is a Tourist Attraction

These exceptions never impinge on the myths. In the service of the redemptive legend of Anne Frank, there is a pattern of pilgrimage to 263 Prinsengracht in Amsterdam. People go to Anne Frank's house to have contact with a consecrated space of suffering. The Dutch are somewhat appalled that the Anne Frank House is such an attraction for tourists—especially for Americans who pay homage to Holocaust remembrance. Nonetheless, this flood of attention is a convenience and a distraction for the Dutch—as well as a lucrative source of income. Tourists don't dig deeper into the history, and the Dutch don't push the matter. Few of the visitors explore what happened to the rest of Dutch Jewry and to the Dutch themselves. There are 800,000 visitors annually at the Anne Frank House, but only 19,000 visit the Hollandse Schouwburg, the former theatre—now a museum and a monument—where the Germans processed many Dutch Jews for deportation.

There is a clear irony here. The 1950s public, including the Dutch, welcomed Anne Frank's miraculously preserved diary. But had she herself returned, few in the Netherlands would have wanted to learn about her suffering. Testimony was not in style. After enduring the occupation and the impoverishment of both the economy and public morale, the Dutch didn't want to hear about the orderly disappearance of 11,000 Jews between 1942 and 1944. . . .

Anne Frank's Diary Is a Significant Contribution to the Literature of Atrocity

Nigel A. Caplan

Nigel A. Caplan is an assistant professor in the English Language Institute at the University of Delaware. His publications include essays and conference proceedings about second-language writers and their work.

According to Caplan in the following selection, Anne Frank's diary has come to exist in three forms: the original version of her diary; her partially revised version, which was likely intended for postwar publication; and the English-language edition published in 1952. A reading across all three versions, asserts Caplan, provides a deeper look into Anne's writing, revealing its merit as a significant element of the literature of atrocity. This viewpoint is in contrast to what Caplan regards as the trend to dismiss the diary as a coming of age story written by an adolescent. Instead, Caplan finds Anne's thoughts were never far from the terror of discovery and persecution by the Nazis. The Franks's seemingly ordinary life was a veneer that allowed them to cope with the reality of their circumstances.

The weighty *Critical Edition* [of *The Diary of Anne Frank*] includes ... Anne's personal diary (the "a-text" found in a diary and two exercise books), her incomplete revision, almost certainly intended for publication after the war (the "b-text," written on typing paper), and the first English-language edition of 1952 (the "c-text"). We can now therefore glimpse what Anne intended us to read, and analyze the strategies she

Nigel A. Caplan, "Revisiting the *Diary*: Rereading Anne Frank's Rewriting," *Lion and the Unicorn*, vol. 28, no. 1, January 2004, pp. 77–95. Copyright © 2004 by The John Hopkins University Press. Reprinted by permission of the editor of Lion and the Unicorn.

employed in her rewriting. By reading the *Critical Edition* both synchronically (across the three versions) and diachronically (through the three versions independently), we can "hear deep in" to Anne's writing, and engage with this text as a significant piece of the literature of atrocity.

Anne began keeping her journal in the plaid-covered diary she was given for her thirteenth birthday; less than a month later, on July 5, 1942, the Franks went into hiding to escape deportation. The first book was filled by the end of November, although Anne periodically returned to add comments and fill in blank pages. The second volume of her original diary, covering the subsequent twelve-month period, has never been found and is presumed lost amidst the chaos of the Franks' capture. On December 22, 1943, Anne continued her diary in an exercise book, which lasted until April 17, 1943, and then began the exercise book in which she would make her very last entry, on August 1, 1944.

Rewriting for Future Publication

On March 29, 1944, after hearing Gerrit Bolkstein, Minister for Education, Art and Science of the Dutch government in exile, announce on Radio Oranje that "after the war a collection would be made of diaries and letters dealing with the war," Anne began to consider writing—according to the most widely read translation—a "romance of the 'Secret Annexe.'" However, the original Dutch word *roman* is a "romance" only in the sense of an imaginative prose narrative: that is, a novel. *Het Achterhuis* [Anne's original title] literally means "the house behind," but translators have generally considered "the Secret Annexe" to be the best approximation. Only the Dutch edition used Anne's own title for her book, whereas by calling it a "diary," translators and critics have either shied away from the implication that they are dealing with a crafted work of literature, or (probably unwittingly) have perpetuated Anne's own fiction of a day-to-day journal.

That the published book is to some extent fictitious is evident in Anne's rereading and rewriting, as she turns a private diary into a public document. . . .

The b-text that she now begins to write opens with a letter to "Kitty" dated June 20, 1942, and ends on March 27, 1944 (which, incidentally, means that at least the revised version of the missing second volume of the diary has been preserved). The proximity of this date to Bolkstein's broadcast two days later may be a sad coincidence. . . .

Both a Personal and Historical Record

The text that Anne Frank envisaged was to be both a personal statement and a record of the circumstances of her life. . . . This raises the thorny issue of whether the literature of atrocity can teach children about that which it describes. . . .

The *Critical Edition* thus sets the *Diary* in a no-man's-land between fiction and memoir. Anne Frank does not fit [literary critic Adrienne] Kertzer's description of "the memoirist [who] often claims that she does not comprehend her own experience. How then can she take on the explanatory function so necessary to the child protagonist who often narrates Holocaust fiction for children?" Anne does understand and explain her own experience, but she writes without knowing for certain the end of her story, and without attempting to interpret what happens beyond the secret annex. . . .

The Holocaust Is Ever-Present in the Diary

As well as drawing the reader into the text, Anne also turns her personal diary into a public document, as the minister had requested. Critics such as [Lawrence] Langer and [Ed] Sullivan have complained that the *Diary* does not venture beyond 263 Prinsengracht [the location of their hiding place], and that the horrors of Nazi persecution remain peripheral to the book. However, the Holocaust is ever-present in the *Diary*. . . . As [essayist] Victoria Stewart has recently argued:

A display of the foreign editions of The Diary of a Young Girl. *Anne Frank's diary has been translated into more than sixty languages worldwide.* © Todd Gipstein/Corbis.

The familiarity of family rows, exchanging of birthday presents, and Anne Frank's hopes and desires is inevitably set against the most unfamiliar series of events, the Holocaust, and it is the ever-threatened eruption of the Holocaust into daily life which *must* give the reader pause.

It is precisely because Anne's life was "pseudo-ordinary" that its representation, the *Diary*, is viable as Holocaust literature. This quotation, though, highlights the limitations of text-based literary criticism, which is uncomfortable with real readers. It is impossible to predict with such certainty how individual readers will respond to any text. In the reader-response tradition, we look for clues in the text which "guide and gauge" the reader's experience.

Anne Turns Her Diary into a Public Text

We can see this guiding hand in the techniques Anne uses to turn her personal diary into a public text. First, she changes her presentation of the unseen horror, which always threatens to erupt into the secret annex. Originally, she listed all the anti-Jewish laws in one long paragraph; this passage was included in the published version, appended to the entry for June 20, 1942. However, in the rewritten b-text for that date, Anne provides a much neater summary of "recent" events in Holland (writing with the benefits of hindsight and the BBC [British Broadcasting Corporation]), which concludes:

> After May 1940 good times rapidly fled, first the war, then the capitulation, followed by the German invasion which is when the sufferings of us Jews really began. Anti-Jewish decrees followed each other in quick succession and our freedom was seriously limited. Yet things were still bearable, despite the star, separate schools, curfew, etc, etc.

Subsequently, though, Anne reincorporates the anti-Semitic laws she has excised here. The effect is subtler, and does not run the risk of disengaging readers by presenting them with a catalogue of misery, but instead provides several brilliantly orchestrated moments which might give anyone pause.

For example, we learn that Jews' access to certain stores has been limited when Anne and her friends go to "the nearest ice-cream shop, Oasis or Delphi, where Jews are allowed." The interdiction on public transport is incorporated into her inserted b-text letter for June 24, 1942 (trams are "a forbidden luxury for Jews"); on July 5, she adds that Jews have to go to special schools and she adds these poignant words to the revised entry describing how her family walked through the rain from their comfortable home to the cramped hiding place:

> We got very sympathetic looks from people on their way to work. You could see by their faces how sorry they were they couldn't offer us a lift, the gaudy yellow star spoke for itself.

Entries Record Her Inner Life

A second strand of Anne's attempt to widen the scope of the diary and thereby be "useful" is in her treatment of politics and the war effort. Largely absent from her personal diary until Bolkstein's radio broadcast, the outside world makes its presence felt more in the b-text and in the later a-text entries through regular war reports, which become noticeably more frequent after D-Day [June 6, 1944]. Often, though, the focus of these entries is not on the events themselves, but on her own feelings and the reactions of those around her, as they ebb and flow with the Allies' progress. Anne was clearly not trying to write a historical document; her focus is inwards, not outwards. . . .

The b-text strikes a delicate balance between the author's dual aims of being useful and giving pleasure. However, it would be inappropriate to conclude that "Anne pulls the reader into her culture each time she begins an entry for a vicarious experience that ends when she signs off in a manner that establishes her immediate presence" [in the words of critic Barbara Chiarello]. Reading *Het Achterhuis* can in no way be described as living vicariously through the fear, discomfort and ever-present threat of capture and death which characterized the Franks' life in hiding. . . .

Anne's Future Becomes Our Past

Alongside her ideals, Anne is fully aware of the "grim reality" (a phrase she uses earlier in this entry) of "confusion, misery and death." Today we know that the very existence of the diary in its present form is predicated on the murder of its author, and the fact that the "approaching thunder" reached her before it could all "come right" makes these words chillingly prophetic. "Perhaps the time will come" is not an expression of childish innocence, optimism and ignorance; it is an adolescent's highly qualified faith. Once we realize that the future she predicts is our past, we can make connections between the text and the world that can be "useful." . . .

The *Critical Edition* reveals some of the strategies that Anne appears to have employed when rewriting her diary for publication. Her revised b-text guides the reader in an attempt

Anne Frank's Diary Is Not a Major Holocaust Text

Lawrence Langer

Lawrence Langer is considered the leading scholar of Holocaust literature and testimony. He has published extensively on the subject, including Holocaust Testimonies, *which was named one of the ten best books of 1991 by the* New York Times Book Review. *Langer is Alumnae Chair Professor of English Emeritus at Simmons College in Boston, Massachusetts.*

In the following essay, Lawrence Langer takes issue with those who promote the belief that Anne Frank's diary makes a major contribution to Holocaust literature. He states that Anne's experience does not represent the archetypal Holocaust experience and that those who have elevated Anne to an icon do her a disservice. In fact, he states that Anne herself would be appalled at how her diary has been misconstrued and her statements—such as the famous "I still believe, in spite of everything, that people are truly good at heart" quote—taken out of context. Langer views Anne's writing as the thoughts of a young girl becoming an adolescent, rather than a record of wisdom and spiritual insight.

In a recent review in *The New York Times* of the . . . "definitive" edition of Anne Frank's *Diary of a Young Girl*, the reviewer calls the work "the single most compelling account of the Holocaust." Nothing could be further from the truth. Anyone familiar with the detailed memoirs of this grim event by Elie Wiesel, Alexander Donat, Filip Miller, Charlotte Delbo and dozens of others must wonder at the spirit of naivete, not to say covert denial, that continues to classify Anne's innocent diary as a major Holocaust text.

Lawrence Langer, "The Uses—and Misuses—of a Young Girl's Diary," *Forward*, vol. 1, no. 5, March 17, 1995.

The Diary of a Young Girl; the Definitive Edition, . . . published by Doubleday, contains 30% more material than the original version, first published in 1947. Readers familiar with the scholarly "Critical Edition" of 1989 will find nothing new. Those unfamiliar with that edition will encounter several explicit allusions to Anne's sexual awakening, expunged by a prudish Dutch publisher, and numerous disparaging remarks about her mother and other inhabitants of the hiding place, which her father decided to censor. These additions do little to alter our image of a gifted young girl who has been inflated into a figure of mythic proportions by an adoring public who never knew her as she really was.

Anne Herself Would Disapprove

I am convinced that if Anne Frank could return from among the murdered, she would be appalled at the misuse to which her journal entries had been put. Above all, her journey via Westerbork and Auschwitz to Bergen-Belsen, where she died miserably of typhus and malnutrition, would have led her to regret writing the single sentimental line by which she is most remembered, even by admirers who have never read the Diary: "I still believe, in spite of everything, that people are truly good at heart." What, she might have asked, of my other views? For example: "There's a destructive urge in people, the urge to rage, murder and kill."

Like many other adolescents, Anne Frank was a creature of moods, shifting attitudes as befit her mercurial temperament. A few lines following the above gloomy commentary, she could write: "I look upon our life in hiding as an interesting adventure, full of danger and romance." How can any mature mind accept this as a serious reflection of the Holocaust experience? Thousands of Jews who spent the war hiding in chilly attics and barns, or in pits which they shared with ground water and rats, cold, hungry, and alone, would be stunned to learn that such an ordeal might be labeled an "interesting adventure."

Sheltering Readers from the Real Holocaust

Anne Frank's experience was distinct, not representative, and those who canonize her as an archetypal victim and use her story to reflect the anguish of an entire people are guilty of a double injustice—to her, and to the millions of other victims. Of the two Annes who exist in the diary, one filled with foreboding and the other unable to suppress her love of life, neither could imagine the atrocities she would be exposed to once she left her attic sanctuary. One appeal of the diary is that it shelters both students and teachers from the worst, to say nothing of the unthinkable, making them feel that they have encountered the Holocaust without being threatened by intolerable images.

Anne Frank herself is to blame for none of this. She knew that the Dutch Jews were being deported somewhere, and that BBC [British Broadcasting Company] news broadcasts mentioned their being gassed, but she never intended her diary to be concerned primarily with the plight of the Jews. Less than 20% of its text is involved with this subject. Anne was proud of her Jewishness, but she did not practice its rituals. She and the other inhabitants of the secret annex celebrated St. Nicholas Day with much greater enthusiasm than they lit Chanukah candles, and in more than two years of entries, she never mentioned the celebration of Passover at all. As for the fate that lay before her and the others should they be discovered, aside from the rumors about "gassing" she had no idea what shape it might take. Indeed, in the Diary itself she is far more frightened by the periodic air raids over Amsterdam than by the prospect of being caught.

A Reflection of Her Growth into Adolescence

It is certainly time to recognize Anne Frank's literary achievement for what it was—not as a source of important information about the Holocaust, but the unfolding of a particular feminine self. The additional material in the new translation, already familiar to readers of the Critical Edition, confirms this view. Moving through puberty into adolescence, Anne captured with a remarkable precocity and sharpness of observation the physical and psychological tensions that are natural to that rite of passage. As the months pass, her entries surge to higher and keener plateaus of understanding, and had she lived, I have no doubt that she would have become a renowned journalist, and perhaps novelist too. Her literary style was mature beyond her years, but this has led some of her most enthusiastic admirers to expect more than she was capable of.

Wisdom and spiritual insight rarely fall from the lips of a 13- or 14-year-old girl. Indeed, as many of the new entries in the diary will show, Anne Frank was essentially a physical being, a lover of nature, intrigued with her own sexuality. Students and teachers should continue to read this unusual diary, but for the right reasons. A wrong one is to consider it a vital text about the doom of European Jewry.

Anne Frank's Story Is Not Remarkable Among Victims of Genocide

Alvin H. Rosenfeld

Alvin H. Rosenfeld, a noted Holocaust scholar, is a professor of English and holds the Irving M. Glazer Chair in Jewish Studies at Indiana University. He is also the director of the university's Institute for the Study of Contemporary Antisemitism.

In the essay that follows, Rosenfeld promotes the idea that, taken in context, Anne Frank's story is not remarkable. She was just one of more than a million Jewish children who were murdered by the Nazis and their allies. Her story takes place far from the locations where most Jews were murdered, and Anne was shielded, says Rosenfeld, from the most horrifying aspects of Nazi terrorism. Anne's story is appealing because it does not describe her eventual fate, so readers are not aware of the horrific circumstances of her death. Further, states Rosenfeld, her story has been "de-Judaized" in that it does not focus on her Jewishness or religious practices. Readers can come away believing they know about the Holocaust without encountering the grim realities of Nazi death camps.

Seen within the context of its time and place, the story of Anne Frank is, sadly, unremarkable. At least a million and possibly as many as a million and a half Jewish children were murdered by the Nazis and their allies during World War II. What distinguishes Annes Frank's story from that of these other children, therefore, is not her early death but the diary entries she kept during the last years of her life and the nature

Alvin H. Rosenfeld, "Anne Frank—and Us: Finding the Right Words," in *Anne Frank: Reflections on Her Life and Legacy*, ed. Hyman Aaron Enzer and Sandra Solotaroff-Enzer. University of Illinois Press, 2000, pp. 207–12. Reproduced by permission.

of the public response to her writings. As we know from the literature that has come down to us from that time, other children likewise kept diaries. But none has been embraced with anything like the interest and affection that Anne Frank's posthumously published diary has received. . . .

It is no exaggeration to say that Anne Frank is probably the best known child of the twentieth century and, as an especially cherished figure, has taken on a symbolic stature almost without rival in the postwar period.

Most Readers Unaware of Anne's Fate

What, though, is the symbolic character of Anne Frank's story? And what explains its continuing popularity? Why is it that she, and almost she alone, stands out among the million or more Jewish children murdered by the Nazis? Does she— indeed, can she—fairly represent the fate of these others? The answer to this last question, unsurprisingly, is no. Her tale, set as it is in Amsterdam, unfolded far away from the places in eastern Europe where most Jews were murdered. During the time when she was hidden in her secret annex, Anne Frank was shielded from the worst aspects of the Nazi terror and knew about them only distantly. It's true that ultimately she came to share the fate of millions of other Jews in the Nazi camp system, but inasmuch as her diary stops before this final, grim chapter of her story, most readers are unaware of the actual circumstances of her end. . . .

Anne's Story Stripped of Its Jewish-ness

[The] image of the emaciated, disease-ridden girl lying dead amidst the human waste of the camp latrine, then dumped into a huge hole that serves as a mass grave, forms no part of the cherished "legacy" of Anne Frank. And yet precisely this was Anne Frank's fate, as it was the fate of innumerable other Jewish victims of Nazi Germany. Following prescribed norms, however, the image of Anne Frank that has evolved over the years has been largely sanitized of any realistic sense of her life and death. Her life has been idealized to the point where it can be summed up by a single, often quoted sentence from the diary—"In spite of everything I still believe that people are really good at heart"—and her death is either glossed over or given a hopeful, even beatific character. . . .

Indeed, it may well be the case that Anne Frank's popularity is owing to the fact that her story remains only imperfectly known and, by and large, has also been "de-Judaized." What remains, although certainly moving, is relatively mild, given what one finds elsewhere in Holocaust literature. No doubt it is for this reason that Anne Frank's story attracts the attention of the young especially and evokes in them a pathos that is vaguely linked to a sense of their own lives, in particular those aspects of their lives that they understand in terms of youthful aspirations and sorrows. Understood in these terms, Anne Frank reflects the familiar personal fears, frustrations, and yearnings of the average teenager. She is bright, eager, energetic, idealistic, romantic—a young girl on the verge of womanhood and a future life of new sensations and satisfactions. . . . She lives in hope, but also in real danger. In all of these respects, she reflects in dramatic form the common teenage fantasies of desire and dread, both of which commingle intimately in her story. They help to account for its immense popularity, not only among the young but, in fact, among all those who retain in adulthood the longings and apprehensions of their youth.

Anne's Readers Shielded from Reality

Anne Frank's tale draws a vast audience to the private life of an admirable young girl but at the same time shields it from a closer knowledge of the brutal fate she shared with millions of other European Jews. By learning the little [that] one comes to learn about the Nazi crimes through the story of Anne Frank, one can "know about" the Holocaust in some distant,

Workers bury bodies in a mass grave at Bergen-Belsen concentration camp in 1945. Anne Frank and her sister, Margot, died from typhus at Bergen-Belsen in March 1945, just two weeks before the camp was liberated. © Bettmann/Corbis.

preliminary way, yet keep from confronting the Nazi horrors at their worst. Furthermore—and this point is crucial—one can embrace Anne Frank as an attractive symbol of youthful idealism and even of martyrdom without recognizing her story as a specifically *Jewish story.* She certainly knew herself as a Jew and was not hesitant to record in her diary some unusually thoughtful reflections on Judaism and Jewish historical fate. But her image has been reconstructed over the past four decades in more neutral terms, and much of her appeal today lies in the vague, universalistic qualities that now surround her story.

Thanks to Broadway and Hollywood, which have projected to millions an Anne Frank who has come to resemble the sweet and lovable girl next door, hers is a story that renders the worst aspects of the Holocaust in grossly understated terms. It is, therefore, a story easy to take. The interpretive stress typically falls on the romantic Anne Frank, the writer Anne Frank, the witty, appealing, and adorable Anne Frank, but rarely on the Anne Frank who would end up as one more anonymous Jewish corpse in the mass graves of Bergen-Belsen. Hounded by her former countrymen as a Jew and placed under a death sentence for the same reason, she has been largely stripped of that part of her identity in her posthumous career as a cultural icon. In this respect she has gone the way of other Jews who have been taken up as culture heroes. . . .

Younger Germans Know Little of Jewish Victims

A whole generation of Germans in the postwar period . . . were raised without much knowledge of the Jewish victims of their parents and grandparents. Anne Frank was either unknown to them altogether or was presented in the hollow terms described above—as a pretty but otherwise non-descript Dutch girl, whose story was moving for its sadness. But the thinking of young Germans in the years following the end of World War II was typically not encouraged to go beyond that point.

Many American Jewish Writers Also Idealize Anne

The slide toward simplification and stereotype is hardly attributable, however, only to the Germans. One finds plenty of others thinking along lines that likewise tend to reduce a complex history to the simple and the stereotypical. A number of the essays collected in David Rosenberg's *Testimony: Contemporary Writers Make the Holocaust Personal* (1989) refer to

Anne Frank, for instance, but do so in ways that demonstrate just how weakened a figure she has become.

Rosenberg asked his contributors, most of them American Jewish writers born during or after the war years, to describe "the shadow of the Holocaust" on their lives. Furthermore, he wanted them to state how and when they first learned of the Holocaust and how it has shaped or been absent from their careers as writers. These are challenging questions, but many of the responses are disappointingly shallow.

Francine Prose, one of Rosenberg's contributors, cites *The Diary of a Young Girl* as an early formative influence on her and remarks that, as a young girl, she read the book again and again. What did it tell her? "For me," she writes, "the book was the story of a girl who had a love affair and a girl who died, and in retrospect I am not sure I knew the difference. . . . I think that I would have been willing to suffer the death if I could have had the romance." Prose writes about the links she felt between herself as a young girl and Anne Frank ("Anne Frank, our sister, our double") and remembers the Holocaust as a focal point for the voluptuous commingling of sex and death. "And so," she notes, "the Holocaust for me became invested with an air of the romantic. It was terrible and glamorous, dark-toned and nostalgic." Whatever else these words may say, they register almost no sense of the extreme character of the events that unfolded in Europe two generations ago. . . .

A Troubling Trend

Following [such] examples, one realizes that the conceptual problem with which we began remains, for to look at the Holocaust "one, by one, by one" [in the words of journalist Judith Miller] is not necessarily to see it clearly. In the case of the popularization of Anne Frank, in fact, a far greater part of this history may be kept from view than revealed. To be sure, there are others who regard the crimes of the Third Reich in more sober and responsible ways, but tendencies to "personalize" or politicize the Holocaust are prominent today and represent a cultural trend that is troubling. It is a trend that has the effect of either denying the realities of Auschwitz or transmuting them into something else—erotic indulgences of various sorts or political action programs that dramatize their appeals through emotionally linked references to the Nazi campaign of genocide. The citations from *Testimony* given above illustrate the former. As an illustration of the latter, one need only look at the rhetoric routinely employed in the debates about abortion and AIDS to realize that "genocide" and "Holocaust" are terms that are being applied to social realities that, for all their gravity, do not resemble the Nazi crimes against the Jews.

Mere Figures of Speech

Those crimes had genocide as their aim and the organized force of a powerful state to implement them in a determined, systematic way. With respect to both intentionality and means, therefore, the Nazi Holocaust was something uniquely evil. An event without identifiable historical precedent, it does not lend itself very readily to comparison or analogy. To say as much is obviously not to say that there are no people today who are suffering, for every day's news shows us that the opposite is true. Nor is it to suggest that we have succeeded in eliminating from our society the various forms of prejudice, intolerance, and injustice that are at the root of so much personal and collective pain, for clearly we have not. However, it is to say that we are likely to obscure rather than to clarify the nature and causes of present-day suffering when we see it as a new form of "genocide" or as the precursor of a second "Holocaust." At the same time, when every instance of human suffering is transfigured as another "Holocaust," the Holocaust itself tends to lose its reality and becomes little more than a figure of speech—its moral claims upon us diminished rather than enlarged by metaphorical extension. . . .

On the other end of the political spectrum, one finds troubling tendencies of another sort. Those of the Left typically do not seek to attack or suppress the historical memory of the Holocaust, but they are disposed to instrumentalize it for their own political ends. In the 1960s, for instance, it was common practice for the figure of Anne Frank to be pressed into service in the struggle against "fascism." There was a time during the Vietnam war when the Anne Frank House in Amsterdam itself became a prominent focal point for the "antifascist" campaign, which, among other things, sought to expose visitors on the Prinsengracht [the street where the Annex was located] to vivid denunciations of the United States as a successor to Nazi Germany. . . .

Given such practices, one worries that the future memory of the Holocaust may become increasingly tenuous. Indeed, since it has entered the domain of public speech, *Holocaust* has become a highly elastic and highly charged figure of speech and is commonly invoked in the debates that are currently raging about abortion, AIDS, civil rights, gay rights, pornography, etc. These are serious debates, but they spring from a history that does not resemble the history that produced Auschwitz and Bergen-Belsen. They have nothing intrinsically to do with Anne Frank or the other victims of Nazi genocide, and we do no honor to Anne Frank's memory or the memories of so many others like her when we see ourselves as "victims" in their image. In fact, it is our good fortune that we are not Anne Frank's "sister" or "double," and we shouldn't pretend to be.

Anne's Diary Illustrates How Hiding Made Familiar Experiences Strange and Scary

Victoria Stewart

Victoria Stewart is a senior lecturer in the School of English at the University of Leicester in England as well as an associate member of the Stanley Burton Centre for Holocaust Studies at the university. She has published Narratives of Memory: British Writing of the 1940s *and* Women's Autobiography: War and Trauma.

In Stewart's assessment in the following selection, Anne Frank's diary is replete with the contradictions of normal human existence and the dangers of exile and discovery by the Nazis. The issue of being a Jew in Holland is set against the backdrop of how, if/when the war ends, Anne and her family can return to everyday life. The Jewish ghetto is not a real community, Stewart explains, but an imposed one. The Annex itself seems to become haunted, and living in a "home" without doors is eerie—a constant reminder of the possibility of death. Familiar activities, such as the constant retelling of the same stories by her elders, become strange and serve to estrange Anne further from the family unit, Stewart asserts.

Even in its early draft, the diary [*The Diary of A Young Girl*] is not solely the record of day-to-day events but also invokes other conventions of autobiography, not least because, as I have indicated, [Anne] Frank details her genealogy, ostensibly for the benefit of Kitty. The history of the family prior to the start of the war is a history of displacement; Anne and her older sister Margot were both born in Germany and the fam-

Victoria Stewart, "Anne Frank: The War from the Annexe," in *Women's Autobiography: War and Trauma*. Palgrave Macmillan, 2011, pp. 84–109. Reproduced by permission.

ily only moved to Holland in 1933. Especially as the war progresses, this complicates not only Frank's sense of her own identity within the family group but also her sense of their religious and national affiliations. Indeed, these two factors are implicated in each other and it is useful to consider Frank's own understanding and projection of her Jewishness in the context of her comments on her national identity. . . .

Jewish Identity Has Negative Connotations

It is only as her anxieties about attitudes towards Jews in Holland grow that she increasingly falls back on her Jewishness as a means of self-definition. Shortly before D-day brings renewed hope of an end to the conflict rumours of an anti-Semitic backlash provoke further reflections on the issue of nationality. Frank records that there are suggestions, in 'underground circles', that German Jews who emigrated to Holland before the war should be sent back to Germany once Hitler is defeated:

> We too will have to shoulder our bundles and move on, away from this beautiful country, which once so kindly took us in and now turns its back on us. I love Holland. Once I hoped it would be a fatherland to me, since I had lost my own. And I hope so still! (*Definitive Edition*, pp. 300–1)

De Costa cites this passage as evidence that, '[t]he position of exile was one of the most dominant aspects of the life and work of Anne Frank' ('Anne Frank', p. 215). Frank understands that it will be impossible to simply leave the Annexe and return to normality, as though awakening from a state of suspended animation. The Annexe dwellers are not only sequestered from the outside world, incapable of effecting changes in their own economic or political situation but are also subject to the exigencies of the type of public opinion Frank describes. Having felt 'at home', albeit in an increasingly segregated Holland, Frank realizes the impossibility of return-ing to Germany. The only option would be a further stage of exile.

'We too will have to shoulder our bundles': the image evoked here is that of the wandering Jew, eternally displaced and never able to assimilate. In later life, Otto Frank described himself as a political rather than religious Jew, but as I have noted, defining oneself was, during the war, secondary to the effects of interpellation. By the time she began the diary, Frank had already had to move to an all-Jewish school, and . . . , she describes the impact of the anti-Jewish decrees. After listing many of the restrictions imposed, she comments, 'Jacque [a schoolfriend] always said to me, "I don't dare do anything any more, 'cause I'm afraid it's not allowed"' (Frank, *Definitive Edition*, p. 8). To be Jewish is to be marked as Other; in this context it is an identity defined by restrictions on one's behaviour. Going into hiding, separating themselves from a society which has stripped away their civil rights is thus, para-doxically, a means of attempting to assert their freedom by depriving themselves of their liberty.

Life in the Annexe Promotes Internal Exile

In view of the Frank family's earlier displacement from Ger-many, the move to the Annexe can be considered as a form of internal exile, during which attempts were made to continue a semblance of everyday life. Two hundred and sixty three Prin-sengracht, where the Annexe was located, became an unheim-lich house, an uncanny double of a family home.

In his study *The Architectural Uncanny: The Modern Unho-mely*, Anthony Vidler returns to a very literal understanding of 'das Unheimliche', but, as its subtitle suggests, Vidler connects this to what is essentially the alienation of modern life. He thus quotes Marx on the estrangement of the individual from his or her home which is the effect of renting property: "'Here I am at home"—but [. . .] instead he finds himself in *someone*

A still from the 1959 film The Diary of Anne Frank. *Victoria Stewart argues that hiding made familiar experiences strange and frightening for the Frank family.* © Time & Life Pictures/Getty Images.

else's house, in the house of a *stranger* who always watches him and throws him out if he does not pay his rent'. Iain Sinclair similarly notes that:

Doors represent status: those who possess them are allowed a measure of privacy. They can remove themselves from their servants, supplicants or creditors. The door is a border, framed and presented. The impoverished [. . .] know them only from the outside. Spaces to which they are granted access have no doors (unless they are doors to keep them in, doors of prisons or madhouses).

Although these observations could, and indeed are intended to, apply to modern life beyond the confines of the Holocaust, their resonance is increased when they are applied to the Annexe. The door to the Frank's 'house' is hidden behind a bookcase. Their ownership of it cannot be freely acknowledged and for much of the time they can make no use of it. When they can, they can only enter other, restricted, parts of the building. This incarceration, as Bettelheim maintains, was chosen, but of course it was barely a choice at all—and was still incarceration. Some of the diary's most tense moments for the present day reader are those when the families have to take precautions not to be heard by workers, or indeed intruders, in the rest of the building. One example of this is Frank's description of the second attempted burglary.

It was ten-thirty, then eleven. Not a sound. [. . .] Up above you could hear the whole family breathing. [. . .] Footsteps in the house, the private office, the kitchen, then. . .on the staircase. All sounds of breathing stopped, eight hearts pounded. Footsteps on the stairs, then a rattling at the bookcase. This moment is indescribable. (Frank, *Definitive Edition*, p. 253)

The Annexe Families' Everyday Life Is Invisible

What such an incident foregrounds for the reader is a usually submerged awareness that the families in the Annexe are carrying out a semblance of everyday life on one side of the wall whilst on the other their presence goes unnoticed. In so far as this is the case, they haunt the building.

On another occasion, after she has been down to the lower part of the Annexe alone to use the lavatory, Frank comments:

> There was no one down there, since they were all listening to the radio. I wanted to be brave, but it was hard. I always feel safer upstairs than in that huge, silent house; when I'm alone with those mysterious muffled sounds from upstairs and the honking of horns in the street, I have to hurry and remind myself where I am to keep from getting the shivers. (*Definitive Edition*, p. 304)

The Empty Building Seems Haunted

Detached temporarily from the family unit, Frank has to remind herself that this is, for the time being her home, and that the 'mysterious muffled sounds', seemingly a sinister threat, are actually being made by her family, who provide her only form of protection. The alternative, signalled by the sound of car horns outside, is a return to the outside world, currently an impossibility. In this passage, the emptiness of the rest of the building is itself a threat, and this, of course is an archetypal trope in the haunted house story. Emptiness and darkness can never be benign absences: there is always a possibility of another presence announcing itself. Even the 'ghosts' can feel themselves to be haunted. Immediately prior to the passage quoted above, Frank prevents herself from considering the possibility that the police, having got into the office downstairs to investigate the break-in, could just have easily have got into the Annexe. What might happen next if such an incursion occurred is not explicitly stated. The fear generated by simply being in the Annexe serves only to mask the fear of what could follow.

Familiar Activities Seem Strange

Here Frank briefly expresses a degree of estrangement from her family. This not only connects to her recurring discussion of the problems of growing up and establishing her own identity in these circumstances but also, perhaps, to a more fundamental sense that the family unit in fact offers little in the way of protection. The sounds she hears are made by her family, but could be made by ghosts. Such defamiliarization is apparent at other points also, in particular when Frank presents images of the older inhabitants of the Annexe. In early 1944, for example, Frank apologises to Kitty for retelling the same news stories, but protests that she herself is 'sick and tired' of 'hearing the same old stuff. [...] Mother or Mrs van D. trot out stories about their childhood that we've heard a thousand times before'.

Such comments have been interpreted as illustrating that the stultification of life in the Annexe ultimately did not dampen Frank's spirits, or as a typical adolescent complaint about her elders. Norma Rosen, for example, sees it as a sign of Frank's 'innate style and unfailing wit' that '[w]hen all the adults in their hiding place grow impatient with her "cheeky" high spirits, this girl so starved for the feel of the outdoors can write: "The rain of rebukes dies down to a light summer drizzle"'. Jenny Diski, meanwhile, suggests that the 'horrible honesty' of Frank's criticism of her mother could be liberating for a teenage reader. But although focusing on how such incidents reveal Frank's creative side (and her desire for the story to continue on the 'right track' could be read as revealing her sense of narrative structure) a particular kind of debilitation is shown to be at work among the adults. Frank might dream of new experiences, but for the older generation, there is a logic in retreating into the past when the future is so uncertain and the present essentially the marking of time. The making-over and retelling of news from outside is a means of absorbing and controlling this information, rendering it non-threatening. Repetition has to take the place of action and becomes a tactic for avoiding the detailed consideration of the present circumstances. This is repetition as a means of masking the loss of one's agency and in this respect it echoes one of the functions of Frank's diary.

Social Issues in Literature

CHAPTER 3

Contemporary
Perspectives on Genocide

India's Aluminum Industry Is a Form of Genocide Against Indigenous People

Felix Padel and Samarendra Das

Felix Padel is an anthropologist trained at Oxford and Delhi Universities. Samarendra Das is an Indian author, filmmaker, and activist. Padel and Das have been researching the Indian aluminum (British spelling: aluminium) industry for a decade. In 2010 they published the book Out of This Earth: East India Adivasis and the Aluminium Cartel.

In the following article, Padel and Das state that the aluminum industry in India, and its impact on the environment and indigenous peoples, amount to a type of genocide. Dams and refineries have displaced many people, and worker deaths at the plants are mostly unreported and uncompensated. The human cost is not included when calculating the "cost" of producing aluminum, the authors claim. Native peoples live sustainably yet have seen their homelands and cultural values destroyed. The human cost will continue for years to come, according to the authors, as fertile lands and forests are exploited for their mineral wealth and the cultures of indigenous peoples are subjected to "ethnicide."

Few people understand aluminium's true form or see its industry as a whole. Hidden from general awareness are its close link with big dams, complex forms of exploitation in the industry's financial structure, and a destructive impact on indigenous society that amounts to a form of genocide. At the other end of the production line, aluminium's highest-price

Felix Padel and Samarendra Das, "Double Death—Aluminum's Links with Genocide," *Economic and Political Weekly*, December 2005. Copyright © 2006 Social Scientist. Reprinted by permission of the editor.

forms consist of complex alloys essential to various 'aerospace'/ 'defence' applications. The metal's high 'strategic importance' is due to its status as a key material supplying the arms industry. In these four dimensions—environmental, economic, social and military—it has some very destructive effects on human life.

The [Indian state of] Orissa Government is presently trying to set up a State-wide programme of rapid industrialization based on a vastly increased scale of mining projects—primarily bauxite, iron-ore, coal and chromite, along with aluminium refineries and smelters, steel plants, plus coal-fired power stations and hydro-electric dams to power them. The idea is that this will rapidly bring great wealth into the State in the form of Foreign Direct Investment, which will quickly pay off Orissa's Foreign Debt to the World Bank and other foreign institutions, at the same time as it promotes overall development in a State which has a high level of poverty and records of starvation deaths. . . .

Dams and Refineries Displaced Many People

In the early 1960s, the Rihand dam was built to supply [Indian aluminum company] Hindalco's refinery-smelter complex at Renukoot (Shaktinagar) on the UP-MP [Uttar Pradesh-Madhya Pradesh] border, displacing a comparable population. None of India's dam projects has kept proper statistics of the people displaced, and none has resettled them adequately. Almost every family of each displaced population suffered a tremendous drop in living standards. The bare estimates of numbers cover a horrendous reality of uprooted communities and human lives reduced to a level of destitution and virtual enslavement. Similar stories surround the Koyna dam in Maharashtra, the Mettur dam in Tamil Nadu, and Korba in Chhattisgarh, which is named after the Korva tribe who were displaced en masse by [Indian aluminum producer] Balco, and whose Census-recorded population shrank from about 84,000 to 27,000 in 1991–2001....

Damanjodi refinery and the upper Kolab dam displaced over 50,000 people, Adivasis [a group of indigenous people] the majority. The rail link between Koraput and Rayagada, built to facilitate Nalco and future aluminium firms, had negative effects on the forest and interior Adivasi villages over a wide area. And Nalco's smelter at Angul has inflicted serious pollution on thousands of people, killing all the fish in a long stretch of the Nandira and Brahmani rivers, as well as killing people and damaging extensive areas of cultivated land when its toxic waste fly-ash ponds have flooded. Tribal villages all around Nalco's bauxite mine on the long summit of Panchpat Mali have suffered pollution and lost their land's former fertility, while over 200 deaths in work accidents at the Damanjodi plant nearby have gone largely unreported and uncompensated, as have deaths from fluoridosis around the Angul smelter, and deaths from industrial pollution among workers in all these plants. So Nalco's high profits come at a huge human and environmental cost that has never been properly calculated—part of the subsidies and 'externalities' of aluminium production we examine below....

The Price of Aluminium Excludes Human Cost

The biggest 'externality' kept out of aluminium's price is the human cost. Mining history in third world countries has always involved a tussle between foreign-controlled companies and the national Governments whose resources are being extracted—a tussle the foreign companies have always won, because they have the close backing of their foreign Governments, each promoting its own economy, and foreign Banks. When Cheddi Jagan in Guyana, [Kwame] Nkruma in Ghana and Michael Manley in Jamaica tried for a little more Government control over the foreign-controlled aluminium industry which dominated their finances, the WB [World Bank] immediately withdrew loans, or threatened to, and their Governments went back to servicing US and British economic interests.

But in this tussle for profits out of mining, what gets left completely out of the picture is the interests of the indigenous people. They get virtually nothing. Only the tiniest percentage of outlay or profits goes on even attempting to compensate them for their dislocation. At first, the company and Govt. authorities say the indigenous people will benefit and raise their standard of living by 'getting developed'. When the people concerned point out their standard of living and quality of life has fallen drastically, a different justification is given: these 'backward' people must pay 'the price of progress'—a 'sacrifice' for the nation's development as a whole.

Destruction, Not Development

This is why Adivasis and those who know them, say these projects are not development at all, but its opposite—a destruction of everything their culture values: land, forest, mountains, flowing water, and the freedom to make their own decisions. Protestors against these projects are often labelled 'anti-development'. But for local communities the industrial projects themselves are anti-development, in the sense of lowering their standard of living.

Government Does Not Assist Displaced People

Government officials in the areas of Orissa affected by rapid industrialization plans, when asked why they don't give Adivasis proper development in the form of schools, hospitals etc, now often reply, 'the company will give this to you': 'Utkal debo', 'Vedanta debo'. This puts people's vital services at the whim of unelected officials of the very companies that are dispossessing them, which then advertise their 'charity' through

A laborer at an aluminum factory in northeastern India in 2010. Felix Padel and Samarendra Das argue that the environmental and economic practices of the aluminum industry amount to a type of genocide against indigenous Indians. © Jayanta Dey/Reuters/Landov.

claims of 'Corporate Social Responsibility'. The human cost behind the bland bureaucratic term 'development-induced displacement' is beyond calculation. All the big 'development' projects mentioned have displaced thousands of Adivasis, and invariably lowered their standard of living to an extreme degree. As [politician and activist] Kishen Pattnayak put this: 'The first step of mining is displacement. In Orissa there is not a single successful story of rehabilitation by the government of displaced families, who otherwise have been surviving on the natural resources of the area by living peacefully since hundreds of years on their own land.'

The social structure of tribal society is inevitably fractured by displacement, as numerous studies have shown. Adivasis know that what is at stake is nothing less than their continued existence as a culture. They live in close-knit communities. Their social values are centred on their relationship with their land and natural environment, and in being self-sufficient for most of their needs by their own labour: for food, building their own houses, etc. To call them 'poor' is correct only when the system of exploitation imposed on them by trader-moneylenders is already taking away a large part of the food they grow. Where they are still largely self-sufficient and control their own land—as in Kucheipadar, and in villages displaced by the Narmada dams—they do not see themselves as poor.

Native People Live Sustainably

The same with moral values: 'We're all saints here' as an elder said to us in a Kond village in Kandhamal District, meaning that everyone in a tribal community lives without excess or wastage, and without trying to accumulate surplus wealth: without the cruel 'competition' that non-tribal society promotes at every level. As true Gandhians [followers of the example and teachings of Mohandas Gandhi], in other words! They see outside society as degenerate and corrupt in the extreme. In particular, they see that projects for their own 'tribal development' have been riddled with corruption, in the hands of non-tribal contractors and officials whose main concern is creaming off their own 'PerCent'. What has been imposed on them already 'in the name of development' is cultural genocide. What right has non-tribal society to speak of 'developing them'? Shouldn't they be developing us, and teaching us the principles of how to live sustainably?

Yet instead of giving tribal culture the respect it deserves, mainstream society still tends to denigrate it, perceiving it through negative stereotypes—'primitive', 'backward', 'ignorant', 'uneducated', 'superstitious', 'lazy' etc.—which actually turn the truth on its head.

The word 'sustainable' sustains considerable abuse nowadays. Almost the only lifestyle that could be defined as really sustainable—over a period of over 2,000 years since [early Indian emperor] Ashoka's time for instance—is one based on communities sustaining themselves through growing their own food, and a strong social structure. Sustainability, in this strict sense, is the essence of Adivasi society. It has sustained itself for centuries through knowledge of appropriate techniques of cultivation and collecting forest produce, not taking too much from nature, and wasting virtually nothing. Present use of terms such as 'sustainable development' and 'sustainable mining' are basically a lie. 'Sustainable' has been narrowed to mean basically 'profitable' over a period of up to about 20 years. What about the next 2,000?

This phrase 'sustainable mining' began to be used from 1999, when the world's 10 biggest mining companies met to launch a project they called 'Mining, Minerals and Sustainable Development' (MMSD, part of their Global Mining Initiative), to see how the mining industry could 'contribute to the global transition to sustainable development'. The long-term vision—how to plan to live sustainably in the long term—is completely absent from the corporate perspective. There is a pervasive blindness to the fact that our limited resources are being permanently destroyed for the sake of short-term gain—that 'current forms of extraction, and the trend for ever-increasing extraction and consumption of mineral products is totally unsustainable'.

Orissa's True Wealth

The main tribe involved in the Orissa Movement, living all around Orissa's bauxite mountains, are the Konds. Their name for themselves is Kuwinga, and they are almost certainly the same people as the Kalinga who fought so hard for their independence against Ashoka's conquest, over 2,000 years ago. The bauxite lies in a layer about a hundred feet thick on top of these 4,000 foot mountains, whose parent rock was named Khondalite by British geologists, since these mountains form the heartland of 'Khond' territory. They also happen to be central to Kond religion and identity. Gopinath Mohanty, in his autobiography, gives a revealing account of a Census official describing to him how some Konds, when asked their religion, replied simply, 'Pahar' (Mountains). The official found this answer absurd, but it actually shows a profound understanding: these bauxite-capped Mountains support abundant plant-life over a wide area, through hundreds of streams that form on their sides. The forest cover, especially when it exists all over a mountain, as with Niyamgiri and Gandhamardan, but also when it is reduced to a small curtain around the rim of the summit, as on Bapla Mali and the other 'deforested' mountains, holds the soil together for these streams to form. The bauxite itself acts as a sponge. It formed here over a period of at least 3 million years, through an annual weathering pattern of alternate rain and sun. Its porous quality makes bauxite ideal for holding the monsoon rain-water over the coming months of the hot season, releasing it slowly through the streams throughout the year, enriched with life-giving trace elements of all the minerals which bauxite is rich in. This is why an abundance of bauxite is probably the main factor in the growth of the world's best tropical and sub-tropical forests, from Orissa to Brazil, north and west Australia, and many other areas.

In other words, Orissa's mineral wealth, certainly in the case of bauxite, is its famed fertility in cultivated land and forest life. Take away the bauxite cappings of these mountains, and Orissa starts to become a desert—a process already visible around Panchpat Mali in Koraput district. For when bauxite is mined out, the mud that is left exposed laterizes and hardens: its previous life-giving properties of storing water etc go into reverse.

Human Cost Includes Future Generations

So the human cost is not only the sacrifice of Adivasi society: it's the sacrifice of future generations of countless Oriyas [citizens of Orissa] yet to be born. What kind of planning destroys all of this for ever for a few years' profit riding the world's currency markets? By contrast, Konds viewing their mountains as Devata [divine]—what could be more realistic and logical? They understand that the mountains give life, in a way that company engineers and certain politicians apparently do not. Even referring to the minerals in these mountains as 'resources' to be 'utilized' brings an ideological distortion. For those living near these mountains, they are not 'resources' but quite simply the sources of life. This is why 'genocide' is an appropriate term for what is happening to Adivasis: a slow death. Not literally the physical death of every individual, as happened in the paradigm case of most of America's or Australia's tribes. But a psychic death: technically, 'ethnicide'— the killing-off of cultures. Without their culture, seeing the sudden confiscation of the land where their ancestors lived and the collapse of their communities, no longer able to grow their own food and forced to eke a living through exhausting and degrading coolie work for the very projects which destroyed their homes, Orissa's displaced Adivasis exist in a living death, witnessing the extermination of all they have valued.

Sri Lanka's Tamils Charge an Army Commander and a US Citizen with Genocide

Bruce Fein

Bruce Fein is an attorney who specializes in constitutional and international law. He was a high-ranking member of the Department of Justice in the administration of President Ronald Reagan. In 2010 Fein published a book titled American Empire Before the Fall.

In this article, Fein, who represents Tamils Against Genocide (TAG), indicts the Sri Lankan defense secretary—a US citizen—and the commander of the Sri Lankan army—a US permanent resident—of 12 counts of genocide and 106 counts of war crimes and torture against the indigenous Tamils. The indictment states that the defendants have been responsible for decimating the Tamil population. The accused are subject to prosecution in US courts under the Genocide Convention of 1948, which was ratified by the US Senate in 1988.

Tamils Against Genocide (TAG) has evidence that 12 counts of the crime of genocide have been committed against the indigenous civilian Tamil population of Sri Lanka outside of any conceivable war or conflict zone, for example, affecting temples, churches, schools, and hospitals. TAG used the legal services of Bruce Fein, Esq. to produce a 3-volume 950+ page model indictment which charges U.S. citizen and Sri Lankan Defense Secretary, Gotabaya Rajapaksa, and U.S. permanent resident and Commander of the Sri Lanka Army, Lt. General Sarath Fonseka, with 12 counts of genocide, and 106 counts

Bruce Fein, "TAG: Executive Summary: Model Indictment Charging US Citizen and Sri Lanka Defense Attorney and US Permanent Resident and Commander of the Sri Lankan Army," *Tamils Against Genocide*, February 17, 2009, pp. 1–4, 6. Copyright © 2009 Tamils Against Genocide. Reprinted by permission of the editor.

of war crimes and torture, in violation of U.S. domestic statutes 18 USC [United States Code] § 1091, 18 USC § 2441, and 18 USC § 2340A.

TAG submitted the model indictment to the U.S. Department of Justice on February 5, 2009 for the US Attorney General to initiate a grand jury investigation aimed at filing a federal criminal case in the U.S. District Court for the Central District of California.

Genocide by US Citizens Is Now a Crime

A recent US statute now makes it a crime for US citizens and permanent residents to be responsible for the crime of genocide committed even outside US borders. If filed, this case would be the first test of the United States Genocide Accountability Act of 2007 sponsored by Senator Richard Durbin (D. Ill.), and supported by then Senators Barack Obama (D. Ill.), Joseph Biden (D. Del.) and Hillary Clinton (D. N.Y.)

The Sinhala-dominated government has discriminated against and persecuted the civilian Tamils of Sri Lanka since independence in 1948. Since the ethnic conflict broke out between the Sri Lankan armed forces and Tamil rebels in 1983, the Tamil areas of the North-East have been subjected to harrowing destruction. The Tamil people there have been indiscriminately killed, disappeared, kidnapped, raped, and otherwise persecuted with the intent to destroy Tamil groups in whole or in substantial part because they are not Sinhalese Buddhists.

US Citizens Indicted

The model indictment organizes all relevant crimes committed against Tamils in Sri Lanka between December 5, 2005 and January 29, 2009. By compiling legal evidence, this document intends to prove that the defendants are individually criminally responsible for genocide, war crimes, and torture as recognized and punishable under U.S. domestic law. Genocide is the deliberate and systematic destruction or attempted destruction, in whole or in substantial part, of an ethnic, racial, religious, or national group, as such. War crimes are the violation of the laws and customs of war and include the murder, ill-treatment or deportation of civilians, the wanton destruction of cities, towns and villages, and any devastation not justified by military necessity.

As detailed in the model indictment, the specific crimes of genocide, war crimes, and torture committed against Tamils during the period from December 5, 2005 to January 29, 2009 (Eelam War IV) [Sri Lankan Civil War], from the rape of Tharshini Illayathamby to the Sencholai school bombing, were committed under the military command responsibility of the defendants through the following non-exhaustive list of methods which were systematically employed in Sri Lanka by the Sri Lankan armed forces and government-sponsored paramilitaries:

> Murder, massacre, torture, mutilation and maiming, disappearance, abduction, rape, gang-rape, sexual abuse and assault, arbitrary or indefinite detention, indiscriminate aerial bombardment, indiscriminate artillery shelling, a permanent cycle of displacement and re-displacement, ethnic cleansing by militarization, colonization and de-population, starvation, deprivation of essential goods, medicine, education and public services, harassment, intimidation, and other stark conditions of life intended to cause the physical destruction of Tamil groups in whole or in substantial part.

Genocide Has Decimated the Tamils

These crimes have brought the Sri Lankan Tamil community close to complete physical destruction, as the model indictment details:

- "Every living Tamil in the Jaffna peninsula and the North-East has been displaced, physically injured,

and/or persecuted by the Sinhalese Buddhist majority—an unprecedented victimization rate approaching 100%."

- "During more than two decades of war, including Eelam War IV, in predominantly Northeastern provincial territories, all Hindu/Christian North-East Sri
  Lankan Tamil villages have been fully depopulated
  at least once." "The economic blockade and military
  attacks worked in tandem with a media blackout,
  and confinement of Tamil civilians in the North-
  East intensified. The GOSL [Government of Sri
  Lanka] continued their genocidal strategy of killing
  Tamils in concentrated locations and imposing
  stringent conditions of life with shortages of food,
  medicine, energy, or housing to destroy Tamils
  physically through starvation, malnutrition, disease,
  and exposure to the elements."

- In one four-year period alone "Sri Lankan forces destroyed 150,000 homes, created six thousand wid-
  ows, orphaned 4,000 children in the North-East,
  damaged 700 temples through bombings, and removed various icons or holy Hindu images from
  sixty-three temples."

- "Poverty, displacement, and garrisoning of entire
  towns and villages by Sri Lanka's armed forces
  caused Jaffna's student population to plunge by
  100,000 since 1995, the Government Agent for the
  northern district reported. Before Eelam III, the
  student population in Jaffna was 240,000. By 2004,
  it had dropped to 140,000."

- "Genocide [was also accomplished] in Jaffna and the
  North-East, respectively, in part through colonization, militarization, and Sinhalization." A population
  which had some of the best indicators of civilian

well-being in South Asia, including literacy and in-
fant mortality rates has now become one of the
poorest areas. For instance, "In 1991, of the total
148,080 tons of essential foods needed in Jaffna,
only 43,080 tons were supplied—a 71% shortfall.
Paddy production plunged 83%." "Before Eelam
War II and the blockade, 700–1000 tons of food
was unloaded annually at Point Pedro Port in
Jaffna; during Eelam War II, that quantity fell to
100 tons." "The fishing sector provided subsistence
and livelihoods for 200,000 Tamils. Annual fish production in this sector fell from 104,300 tons to
1,094 tons, a drop of 98.95%, occasioned by national security restrictions. Local consumption before the blockade annually required 6,605 tons of
fish. Only 16.6% of that tonnage was caught after
1990." In 2002, "[t]he SLA [Sri Lanka Artillery] destroyed 50,000 palmyra palm trees on the route
joining Thalaimannar to Mannar. Approximately
forty thousand Tamil families depend on palmyra
palm plantations while another twenty-five thousand families' livelihood depends on toddy [palm
liquor] production, handicrafts, as well as other tree
products." "In the 10-months from June 1990 to
April 1991, North-Eastern hospitals required 220
million rupees to operate, but the GOSL only supplied 7%—15 million—of the required amount,
and did so irregularly." During the same period,
"Amparai, whose Sinhala population had risen since
independence due to state-sponsored colonization,
received funding and treatment for 90% of their
needs." "In the Jaffna peninsula, for example, the
SLA's Operation Whirlwind in May 1992 bombed 8
hospitals and surrounding infrastructure."

- "The Mannar Bishop and human rights activists lamented [in 1998] that the CSU [Counter Subversive Unit] habitually arrests women such as Sivamani and Wijikala [Tamil women who were in military custody] from various parts of the Mannar district to rape and exploit brutally under the pretext of interrogation and extended detention pursuant to the Prevention of Terrorism Act and the Emergency Regulations."

Tamils Displaced and Murdered

- Colonization of Sinhalese into Tamil areas has continued apace. For instance, "The GOSL began construction of a Buddhist shrine in Vilankulam, a traditional Tamil village in 2002. . . . In a companion act of religious bigotry [nearby, two weeks later], the GOSL banned renovation of the historic Hindu temple at Kanniya, in Trincomalee." In 2007, "[w]hile a majority of the 222 Tamil families from the traditionally all Tamil Raalkuli village in Muthur division in Trincomalee District had been displaced due to SLA and SLAF [Sri Lanka Armed Forces] attacks, by this date, a Colombo-based Buddhist organization laid the foundation stone for 138 houses intended for the settlement of Sinhala-Buddhist civilians in the village."

- "The fact is that not a single member of the security forces had, at the date of the Mission, been convicted of murder. . . . A culture of impunity has developed, with perpetrators of grave violations being convicted of minor offenses or, in most cases, not at all," [according to the] Centre for the Independence of Judges and Lawyers in Geneva, 1997. "Torture has been facilitated by widespread impunity of the perpetrators. To date, no member of the security forces has been brought to justice for committing torture," [according to] Amnesty International, 1998

In the legal argument of the model indictment, the counts of genocide, war crimes, and torture which hold the defendants culpable for crimes committed during Eelam War IV against Tamils are framed within a larger motivational context which preceded the genocide in Eelam War IV, and which details virtually every documented crime committed against Tamils from 1948 to November 2005, including acts of genocide which occurred in Eelam Wars I–III and the recent ceasefire period.

The pre-Eelam War IV motivational context articulates the complexity and gravity of the Tamil genocide and demonstrates that the Tamil genocide as it unfolds in Eelam War IV can neither be interpreted in isolation nor decontextualized from the post-independence pattern of facts and historical events which show the persistent intent of successive democratically elected Sinhala-Buddhist regimes to commit deliberate acts of genocide with the intent to destroy in whole or in substantial part the Hindu/Christian North-East Sri Lankan Tamil national, ethnic, racial, religious group, as such, in the North-East provincial territories of Sri Lanka, which includes the heavily populated Jaffna peninsula.

Genocide vs. Crimes Against Humanity

The difference between genocide and crimes against humanity in their legal definition is that genocide is an intent-based crime; crimes against humanity are not. Proof of genocidal motivation is occasionally direct, as with Defendant Fonseka's assertion that Sri Lanka is a Sinhalese nation—not a multi-ethnic nation. Other evidence of motivation is circumstantial, for example, no Tamils serve in the security forces; and, no Sinhalese Buddhist perpetrator of extra-judicial killings, torture, rape, and other atrocities has ever been both prosecuted and punished in more than 60 years, with one minor exception.

12 counts of genocide are charged in the model indictment, followed by 106 counts of war crimes and torture. These introduce the option of legal action which charges the defendants for acts of war crimes and acts of torture where, unlike the counts of genocide, the proof of intent to physically destroy on whole or in substantial part a Tamil group is not required.

The indictment charges violations of U.S. criminal laws, not international law. The institutions entrusted with enforcing international criminal prohibitions, for instance, the International Criminal Court or the International Court of Justice, are routinely hijacked by big-power politics. China would frustrate any effort to call the Defendants to account before international bodies, just as it has for its own crimes against Tibetans or Uighurs.

Prosecution in US Courts Needed

Recourse is being made to prosecuting these crimes in US courts because the government of Sri Lanka, controlled by the island's Sinhala-Buddhist majority, has been an impediment to delivering any justice for crimes against Tamils in Sri Lanka. Further, the defendants are a U.S. citizen and a U.S. permanent resident, whom the United States has a special responsibility for prosecuting under the Genocide Convention of 1948, which was ratified by the U.S. Senate in 1988. United States courts are fiercely independent, and will not be distracted in a genocide prosecution about arguments over the LTTE [Liberation Tigers of Tamil Eelam, a separatist organization] or other legal irrelevancies to the crime that the defendants would attempt to interject.

In the model indictment, to supplement the sections on the accused and the charges, sections such as evidentiary sources, general allegations, additional facts, and individual criminal responsibility contextualize the counts of genocide, war crimes, and torture. . . .

The History of Tamil Genocide

All previous well-known genocides which have occurred since the end of World War II have been characterized by a massive number of murders in a small defined locality occurring in a short time period and carried out by an actor seeking the total physical extermination of a particular ethnic group. The post-1945 genocide cases often cited are: the Holocaust, Cambodia, the Kurds in Iraq, the Srebrenica massacre [in Bosnia-Herzegovina], Rwanda, and Darfur [in Sudan].

By contrast, Sri Lanka's genocide against Tamils has taken place over a number of years and is more characterized by widespread, prolonged displacement and destruction of the community's physical and cultural base than murder. For this and also wider geopolitical reasons, the destruction of the Sri Lankan Tamils is less well-understood in the world at large as a case of genocide. The model indictment accommodates this lack of awareness into its articulation of the patterns of Tamil genocide.

The 2007 US Genocide Accountability Act defines genocide as an attempt to physically destroy a group in whole or in substantial part because of race, religion, ethnicity, or nationality, as such, by employing the following tactics: extrajudicial killings or disappearances; the infliction of serious bodily harm; or, the creation of conditions of life intended to cause the physical destruction of a racial, religious, ethnical, or national group in whole or in substantial part. The evidence collected and organized in the model indictment proves beyond a reasonable doubt that Eelam War IV is genocide masquerading as counter-insurgency. Every incident of genocide chronicled in the indictment was inflicted on Tamil civilians outside any conceivable war zone and uninvolved in the ethnic conflict between the LTTE and the government.

The central difference between the Tamil genocide and other post-1945 genocides is that in Sri Lanka the culture of genocide seeks to physically destroy Tamils in substantial part, not in whole, if the Tamil survivors are willing to accept vassalage or serfdom to Sinhalese Buddhists.

Women and Children Are Murdered in the Darfur Genocide

Joshua Price

Joshua Price is a writer whose articles appear on www.suite101 .com.

The president of Sudan has declared that the residents of Darfur need to be eliminated, states Price in the selection that follows. The real danger to Darfurians is the Janjaweed militia, whose sole purpose is to inflict terror and death upon them. According to Price, China is supplying weapons and training to the Janjaweed as a ploy to curry favor for Sudan's oil reserves. Women and children are increasingly subjected to rape and torture, especially as more women are forced to become heads of households. Price urges the US government to take action, and many well-known Westerners are working to bring attention to the plight of Darfur.

The word genocide usually conjures up images of the Holocaust. One thinks of walking skeletons in prison uniforms, domes full of human ashes, or pictures of heartless guards brutally gunning down prisoners. But the exact same cruelty is happening now, as these very words are written, in the Darfur region of Sudan. Despite international media and the International Criminal Court condemning it for years, this violence has gone on unopposed for even longer than the Holocaust lasted.

Exterminated for Being Different

In 2003, Omar al-Bashir, president of Sudan, decided that the residents of the Darfur region needed to be wiped out. His reason: they were different. If not for a bit of fortuitous geography, he would have succeeded. Darfur is in western Sudan, along the border with Chad. The Darfuri were able to flee across the border into Chad to escape the first waves of violence.

Upon arrival, the Darfuri set up large refugee camps in the desert. As a desert camp, the refugees endure extreme heat by day and terrible cold at night. The cold nights have made firewood currency.

Janjaweed Militia Attacks Refugee Camps

The real danger and nightmare of the camps is not the elements, but the Janjaweed militia, the brutal arm of the Darfur genocide. The Janjaweed ride in on horses and helicopters at will to spread death. Their instructions are to do exactly that.

In one of his many publications on the Darfur Genocide, Nicholas Kristof of the *New York Times* cites a document in possession of a Janjaweed commander ordering [the militia] to "'Change the demography of Darfur and make it void of African tribes, the document urges. It encourages 'killing, burning villages and farms, terrorizing people, confiscating property from members of African tribes and forcing them from Darfur.'"

China Is Assisting the Janjaweed

The UN troops do little to help, and in any case they are undermanned. The Janjaweed's weapons are supplied by the Chinese. The Chinese have even gone as far as "training fighter pilots who fly Chinese A5 Fantan fighter jets in Darfur."

China's motivation is to jump to the front of the line for Sudan's oil reserves. And since China is on al-Bashir's side, no one wants to anger the Chinese. This is one reason why the world's governments do nothing. The people of Darfur have no resources, or skills-in-trade, or political clout. In international politics it is trade, not human lives, that carries the day.

Increasing Awareness of Darfur

Many prominent Westerners have spearheaded awareness and humanitarian initiatives to help Darfur. [Actress] Mia Farrow, for one, has visited Darfur many times to bring food and document the genocide firsthand. But such efforts are useless in the face of gun-toting soldiers who pillage the donated supplies.

The World Seems Indifferent to Darfur

In 2009, the International Criminal Court issued an arrest warrant for Omar al-Bashir. Incensed, he ordered the Janjaweed to kidnap aid workers. Volunteers from Canada, Ireland and France were snatched from the aid offices.

The world was at a standstill. It seemed that al-Bashir had finally crossed a line the world would not tolerate. But in the end, even threats to their own nationals did not stir the West into action. The world has sent a clear message to the people of Darfur: they are expendable and their lives don't matter.

Women and Children Tortured

The Janjaweed militia have no resistance. Therefore, their hatred and inhumanity can be given full rein. It is not enough for the Janjaweed to murder. They relish in suffering. The following are crimes attributed to the Janjaweed by Nicholas Kristof in his many writings on Darfur.

As young women have become the heads of their families due to the disappearance of the men to the dustbin of war, those young women are the ones who have to venture out for food, water, and firewood. It is outside their tents where they encounter the Janjaweed.

The lucky ones are the ones who are not literally raped to death. Some of the less lucky ones suffer severe genital injuries during their attacks. To prove that their victims are not human and not attractive, the Janjaweed take to burning their victims' breasts so they can never breastfeed again.

Those men who are around suffer just as badly. One man had his eyes gouged out by a bayonet. Others are simply castrated. And men, like the women and children around them, are burned to death.

Children are little more than target practice for the Janjaweed. A common sport is to try to spear multiple children with a single bayonet. Some children are beaten so severely their faces cannot be recognized. There is more horror, but [it is] too graphic to mention.

How Can the Darfur People Be Helped?

For starters, raise awareness. Tell family, friends and coworkers about what is happening. Stay educated. Spread the word about 1-800-GENOCIDE, the toll-free hotline that connects people to their Member of Parliament or Representative in [the US] Senate. Once connected, leave a message urging for action in Darfur.

There are many charities that send aid to Darfur, but aid only does so much when supplies are stolen and workers imperiled. The people of Darfur will only be helped when the world's leaders take action and provide protection.

There is one such leader who is in an excellent position to help Darfur: Barack Obama. President Obama commands the world's most powerful army, his father is African, and he is dripping with diplomatic goodwill. Write him a letter and see if he can be moved to help.

Every donation gives food and water to one starving family. Each additional person who writes to their Representative is one more vote that Representative will want to win. Each additional letter to President Obama makes his staff move Darfur that much higher on his to-do list.

The International Criminal Court Is Ineffective in Stopping Genocide in Africa

Ronald Elly Wanda

Ronald Elly Wanda, a lecturer at Marcus Garvey Pan-Afrikan Institute in Mbale, Uganda, is a writer and political scientist who lives and works in London. His work focuses mainly on political and sociocultural issues that concern and affect Africans.

The International Criminal Court (ICC) was formed to administer justice; however, it has not been effective in resolving legal issues in Africa, asserts Wanda in the following selection. Wanda claims that the ICC operates under the guise of "legal colonialism" in its treatment of African communities due to its Western European mode of delivering justice. However, preconceived hierarchical ideas of European justice do not work within the African tradition of consensus, in the author's view. Wanda further contends that African governments' reliance on foreign financial assistance makes them vulnerable to the interests and priorities of foreign nations.

The beginning of June [2010] saw Uganda's capital Kampala, the heartbeat of Africa, play host to the first ever Review Conference of the Rome Statute, which in 2002 gave birth to the International Criminal Court (ICC). A timely event that triggered a renewed interest in discussions centered on the limits and possibilities of international justice serving African interests. Questions such as: "is there sufficient gravity for Africans to depend on the International Criminal Court (ICC) to deliver local justice?" dominated civil talks at malwa (local brew) dens in towns and villages right across the continent.

In East Africa, the Kenyan Nobel Peace laureate, Wangari Maathai, added to the works. Writing in an East African weekly prior to the conference, and in reference to her native Kenya—which saw 1300 killed and more than half a million internally displaced following the post-election violence of late 2007, she argued that Africa has leaders that make violence against humanity seem worthwhile. "These leaders", Maathai observed, "mobilized their supporters, mostly from their communities, to go and kill and rape and destroy members of other communities". Accordingly, Maathai affirmed that Africans support the ICC in bringing to an end the culture of impunity by holding those who commit such crimes in Africa to account. "Impunity", noted the Professor, "not only perpetuates crimes against women, children and other civilians, it teaches successive generations how to continue the violence".

Unequal Justice in Africa

Whilst it is difficult to fault the professor, my Pan-African impulse is very much enticed. From ancient European philosophers, namely Plato and Aristotle, to notable African thinkers [Cheikh] Anta Diop, [Dani Wadada] Nabudere, [Ali] Mazrui, [Archie] Mafeje and undoubtedly many others, runs a thread of universal agreement that the idea of justice inevitably suggests the notion of certain equality. In Africa this has not been the case.

Given five centuries of systematic destruction of African communities' political, cultural, economic and social structures by Europeans, Africa is yet to attain psychological wellbeing from the sustained assault on its humanity, which continues to this day under different guises now including the ICC's "legal colonialism". Exogenous forces aside, today's societies in Africa are also deeply marked by class, ethnicity, gender, religion and other dimensions of difference and inequalities, making injustice instead of justice the norm. The continent has been forced to continue nursing a deep sense of what my good friend, Professor Mammo Muchie, has termed "wounded psyche" in its memory that keeps attacking the marrow of its social, political as well as its legal confidence.

Western Justice Has Failed

Since flag independence in the 1960s, African governments have been in a rush to normalize authoritarian rule and human rights abuses under the auspices of Maendeleo (development) and economic growth. A short stroll in any African village today confirms that the globalised Western culture of justice delivery or for that matter innovation, that most African leaders seem to trust, has not improved the well-being of our local communities or delivered justice for them. On the contrary, it has often blocked viable indigenous innovation of cultures and suffocated African justice. Here in East Africa, cultures of innovation have largely accrued from the jua kali (informal), and not the formal sector. Indigenous cultural innovations have also been at the centre of development in most Highly Indebted Poor Countries (HIPC) such as in Uganda or her slightly richer sister Kenya, notably because of wanainchi (citizens') exceptionally limited access to capital.

As such, when it comes to delivering justice in Africa, we ought to revise our priorities by doing away with existing preconceived ideas that might have worked within the European cultural setting as they have clearly not acted up in the face of socio-cultural heritage of African societies; neither has the opposite—the Afrikanisation of western concepts of justice delivery.

African Justice Has a Different Approach than Western Modes

This is because the Western justice paradigm remains retributive, hierarchical, adversarial, punitive and is guided by codified laws and written procedures. Whilst on the other hand, African justice systems have always been guided by unwritten

Entrance to the International Criminal Court (ICC) in The Hague, Netherlands. Ronald Elly Wanda argues that the ICC has failed to provide an effective form of justice against the perpetrators of genocide in Africa. © AFP/Getty Images.

laws, traditions and practices like inclusiveness, consultation and consensus. These are learned primarily by example and through the oral teachings of elders. In any legal matter, every adult member of the community gets involved into solving a conflict and they all focus on the need to resolve issues so as to attain peace and social harmony. The community is involved in the entire process; from disclosure of problems, to discussion and resolution, to making amends and restoring relationships.

Recently while on a study visit to Iwokodan, an iteso clan in Kamuge, Pallisa District, north eastern Uganda, I was narrated a story of a land dispute involving two community members that took twenty years being tossed around courts that was eventually resolved within days after it was referred back to the clan. In that case an amicable resolution was reached promptly because of elements such as: the just act is correctness; the rejection of inequality; reason instead of arbitration; conscience instead of inhumanity and so forth that one finds in traditional African justice unlike the existing westernized arrangement. Another example is Rwanda where the re-establishment of its traditional courts (the Gacaca) to help deal with the crime of genocide and foster reconciliation between its communities has yielded a positive outcome.

Out of Touch with Africa's Realities

When it comes to international law, it is fair to argue, African states have failed to abide by their international fair trial obligations probably because these standards have been impractical in the first place, given the realities of poverty, illiteracy and strong cultural beliefs that characterize most of our communities in Africa. As a result, the law applied by the Western-style courts is felt to be so out of touch with the needs of most African communities and coercion to resort to them therefore amounts to denial of justice.

As for the ICC, we must reject it on the basis that it is an epithet of legal colonialism by the European Union (EU). Not only does it receive 60 percent of its funding from the EU, it has also ignored all European or Western human rights abuses in conflicts in Iraq and Afghanistan or human rights abuses by states considered "darlings of the West". Despite over 8,000 complaints about alleged crimes in at least 139 countries, the ICC has started investigations into just five countries, all of them here in Africa. The ICC's double-standards and autistic legal blundering in Africa has derailed delicate peace processes that have instead prolonged devastating civil wars. As Dr David Hoile, author of *The International Criminal Court: Europe's Guantanamo Bay?* has observed, "the court's proceedings ought to be questionable given its judges, some of whom have never been lawyers, let alone judges, [and] are appointed as the result of vote-trading among member states".

Adding, "The ICC has engaged in prosecutorial decisions which should have ended any fair trial because they compromised the integrity of any subsequent process. Its first trial stalled because of judicial decisions to add new charges halfway through proceedings".

African Reliance on Outside Funding Creates Vulnerability

African governments' continued reliance on donor funding has made societies in Africa vulnerable to the vulgar[it]ies of shifting donor conditionalities and (wicked) interests. Malawi's president, Bingu wa Mutharika's recent retract from his 14 year prison sentence of Monjenza and Chimbalanga, a homosexual couple, and Uganda's Yoweri Museveni's disposal of the Anti-Homosexual Bill (the so called Bahati Bill) respectively, serves as points in reference.

Therefore, concerns for the emancipation of the continent from the ravages of foreign domination and underdevelopment and building of a new Africa from the grassroots upwards ought to be a concern for us all. As renowned scholar Dani Nabudere forcefully urges, "we must defend African people's dignity and civilisational achievements and contribute

Christians in Iraq Are Being Killed in Systematic Genocide

Rosie Malek-Yonan

Rosie Malek-Yonan can trace her Assyrian roots back nearly eleven centuries. As an actor, director, and author, she is an activist for the rights of Assyrian Christians in Iraq. Her book The Crimson Field *garnered an invitation to testify before the US Congress about the genocide and persecution of Assyrians in Iraq. She is frequently interviewed on radio and television and was the recipient of the 2009 Assyrian Woman of the Year Award.*

Assyrian Christians are an indigenous minority in war-torn Iraq. Malek-Yonan says in the following article that this population is subject to increasing terrorism and murder by Muslims, including forty-eight churches that were attacked, bombed, or destroyed; kidnappings; and beheadings of Assyrian clergy and children. The February 2008 murder of an Assyrian archbishop was widely condemned and served to bring attention to the plight of this minority. In the author's view, however, the United States has done little to stem the tide of terrorism, in spite of the millions of dollars spent on the Iraq War. Hundreds of thousands of Assyrians have become refugees, fleeing to Syria, Lebanon, and Jordan. Malek-Yonan asserts that unless the United States makes a plan to set aside an Assyrian-administered region in Iraq, this ancient civilization will disappear.

While leaving Mosul's Holy Spirit Cathedral on February 29, 2008, gunmen abducted Archbishop Paulos Faraj Rahho, killing his driver and two bodyguards. Twelve days later, the kidnapped archbishop was found dead, buried in a shallow grave near Mosul.

Rosie Malek-Yonan, "Genocide Unfolding: Death of a Catholic Assyrian Archbishop in Iraq," *Assyrian International News Agency*, March 18, 2008. Copyright © 2008 Assyrian International News Agency. Reproduced by permission.

The widespread condemnation of [the] death of the 65-year-old Assyrian Archbishop of the Chaldean Catholic Church in Mosul, Iraq has been reverberating around the world. From Prince Hassan bin Talal of Jordan to Pope Benedict XVI, the expression of outrage has been heard. There's no shortage of statements issued by various Assyrian, Chaldean and Syriac groups, individuals and journalists. Various Christian groups around the globe have also been lending their voices in support of the Christians in Iraq. Stories of Archbishop Rahho's death streaming the news for the past two weeks clearly attest to the fury.

Pope Benedict XVI issued an urgent request during his Sunday sermon this week [March 2008] to end the massacre in Iraq. Will an abstract plea of peace in Iraq bring about change? Will the Pope's cry of "enough to the violence in Iraq" stop the brutality? Or will the words of the pontiff quickly fade into oblivion by his next Sunday's Vatican sermon? The Pope has made similar pleas in the past that have gone unanswered.

A Lack of US Response

Did the U.S. government show enough concern to quickly and actively look for Archbishop Rahho while he was fighting for his life in the hands of his captors? It was repeatedly reported that he suffered from a heart problem and was dependent upon medication for survival that he was deprived of by his kidnappers.

Clearly the outrage was not enough to prompt the U.S. government to take immediate action while the archbishop was held for ransom.

But what if it had been an American, European, or Israeli abducted for ransom? Would the world have reacted differently?

Assyrians Cannot Fight Terrorism Alone

Alone and abandoned, Iraq's rapidly declining Assyrian Christian nation is left to fend for itself while besieged by daily terror. Unarmed and isolated, this small nation cannot fight the extreme terrorism that is targeting its people. Not even in retaliation do the minority Christians in Iraq strike back against their aggressors. These systematic violent attacks have now turned into a full-blown genocide against the Assyrians, the indigenous people of Iraq that includes the Chaldeans, Syriacs, and all the other various Christian denominations.

With millions of dollars vested in the Iraq War and with all its sophisticated war machinery, the U.S. has no handle on this conflict that has been erupting in the battlefields of Iraq since 2003. How then can an unarmed and unprotected small minority with no funding and no weaponry expect to survive under the same conditions?

After more than four years of deliberate attacks on the Christian population in Iraq, there seems to be a "momentary outrage" about the death of an archbishop. But time and time again, we have witnessed the emergence of a "momentary outrage" that falls short on impulsion. On October 11, 2006, Fr. Paulos Eskandar, a Syrian Orthodox priest was beheaded with his arms and legs hacked off. Surely that crime should have been enough to capture the world's attention and to bring about change in the treatment of the Christians in Iraq.

Protests of Injustice Do Not Last

But how long will these cries of unjust against this latest offense last? Now that Archbishop Rahho had been laid to rest, will he, too, fade from memory like all the others before him? Or will the "momentary outrage" continue long and loud enough for the good citizens of the world to take on a more proactive role to save this nation from extinction? Will President [George W.] Bush have the courage to take off his blinders or will he continue to stumble in the dark until his final day in office?

With every attack on the Christians in Iraq, I ask, "Have we reached the blistering point? Will this be the turning point for the Assyrians?" I usually find my answer when I see the stories rapidly fading.

One of Many Christians Murdered

Certainly the death of Archbishop Rahho is a great tragedy but by no means is it an isolated case and should not over-shadow the systematic and targeted murder of countless other innocent Christians in Iraq.

In June of 2006, my American government, the same government that attacked Iraq, invited me to testify on Capitol Hill [in Washington, DC,] about the persecution of the Assyrians in Iraq since 2003. There was a promise of hope in the air. I witnessed the "momentary outrage" on the part of the members of the Congressional Committee of the 109th Congress I appeared before. My testimony even brought Representative Betty McCollum to tears.

The "momentary outrage" lasted long enough to prompt Congressman Christopher Smith to visit Iraq and meet with Assyrian Christians including Pascal Warda, a former minister in the Iraqi transitional government, and turned in my report to U.S. Officials in Iraq.

Believing [him] to be a man of his word, I have since been holding Congressman Smith accountable for his promise to me when on the record he stated:

"I thank you for that very powerful testimony. I just want you to know that you point out no one's taking notice. The reason why we invited you and wanted you here was to try to begin to rectify that. To raise this issue with our own government and other coalition partners, especially the Iraqis. Your testimony will be used, I can assure you, to try and rectify things."

Congress's Attention Is Ineffective

But even though the atrocities committed against Assyrian Christians were brought to the attention of Washington and my report went full circle when Congressman Smith returned it to the "scene" of the crime, it did not reduce the amount of violence perpetrated against Assyrians in Iraq. On the contrary, the brutality escalated into an unstoppable frenzy while the West continued to turn a blind eye. The promise of hope vanished.

From 2003 to 2008, 48 churches have been attacked, bombed, burned and destroyed. In January 2008, seven simultaneous attacks were made again on churches and monasteries. Assyrian children and clergy beheaded and dismembered. Assyrians kidnapped for ransom and murdered. Young Assyrian boys crucified. Women and young girls raped. Assyrian men and boys tortured. Infants burned. Assyrians intimidated and threatened. Land and property confiscated. Business[es] destroyed. Forced migration in a large-scale exodus from Iraq that at one point escalated to 2,000 Assyrians each day. Muslims carrying out threats of Convert or Die. Forced Islamization by way of Assyrian Christians ordered to pay a *jeziya*, a tax levied on Christians, a practice that is entrenched in ancient Islamic practice. Despite all the crimes against the Assyrians in Iraq, this small nation has continued to remain peaceful, patient and tolerant witnessing its own demise through a modern day ethnic cleansing with the full knowledge of the U.S. and the Coalition Forces, making them silent accomplices to these crimes.

Today's Assyrian Genocide in Iraq is reminiscent of the Assyrian Genocide of 1914–1918 in Ottoman Turkey and northwestern Iran where two-thirds of that nation were exterminated. Silent accomplices to those crimes were plentiful.

Numerous Assyrians Forced to Become Refugees

Since the liberation of Iraq, hundreds of thousands of Assyrians, who were once productive members of society in their homeland in Iraq, have become refugees, stranded and now abandoned in Syria, Lebanon and Jordan. They once owned businesses, homes, communities, schools, and churches. Now they live in absolute poverty, forsaken with no hope on the horizon as they face deportation from those respective countries.

Perhaps Congressman Donald Payne's June 30, 2006 comment on the record to me was more apropos when he stated, "The wheels of justice sometimes grind slowly." In the case of the Assyrians, the wheels of justice have stopped.

In June of 2007, a year after my Congressional Testimony, the U.S. Congress approved a $10 million aid through a Sub-Committee on State and Foreign Operations to assist the minorities in the Nineveh Plain in Northern Iraq, namely the Assyrian Christians. Compared to the destructions of lives brought upon the Assyrians in Iraq by the U.S. invasion, a $10 million aid is a band-aid solution to a much deeper, and far more serious problem.

The Muslim Ultimatum

The Leave or Die message regularly delivered to the Assyrians of Iraq by the Muslims is a daily reminder of the instability the U.S. has created for that Christian nation. Unless an immediate plan is put into action to establish an Assyrian-administered region in Iraq, with a police force drawn from Assyrian towns and villages in the Nineveh Plains, this ancient civilization will without a doubt disappear.

The simple fact is that when the United States, a Christian country, attacked Iraq, it was seen as an attack on Islam. The Assyrian Christians of Iraq including all the various religious denominations have become a target of retribution against the western Christian invaders. The reluctance on the part of the U.S. to save the Christian minorities in Iraq may stem [from] the simple fact that the Muslim Iraqis will view this as the U.S. "helping one of its own." Could this be one of the reason the U.S. government chooses to not deal with this embarrassing disaster?

The Christians in Iraq did not start the war in Iraq. Today they are caught in the line of fire while the U.S. continues to evade the human tragedy of the genocide it is directly responsible for when President Bush first ordered the attack on Iraq.

US Government Responsible

The actions of the U.S. government are nothing less than irresponsible. Why should the Assyrians have to pay the price of this war with such heavy losses? These losses will never be recouped.

As an American citizen and as an Assyrian, I am outraged at the callousness of my government in addressing the predicament it has placed my Assyrian nation in. If the intention of the U.S. is to continue to act as though it does not notice this problem, then before washing its hands completely of the chaos it has created in the Middle-East firstly it must train and arm the Assyrian Christians fully so that they can combat and cope with the daily attacks. Secondly, it is imperative that the U.S. and Iraqi governments immediately deal with the Assyrian issue in the same manner as they did in dealing with the Kurds back in 1991 [following anti-government rebellions], by establishing an "Assyrian Safe-Zone." With the help of the United Nations, the prosperity of this region can slowly begin, and perhaps finally the Assyrians will be able to once again become a thriving nation on their own, much like the Kurds.

Many Children Were Murdered or Orphaned in Rwanda's Genocide

UNICEF

UNICEF is the United Nations Children's Fund, which works for children's rights, development, and protection. UNICEF was established by the United Nations in 1946. US funding for UNICEF helps children in 150 countries.

UNICEF reports in the following report that the children of Rwanda continue to suffer the effects of the genocide in their nation, which ended in 1994. All told, 800,000 people were murdered, and 300,000 of that number were children. Further, 95,000 children were orphaned. These children witnessed and/or were victims of brutality and terror, the viewpoint claims. Some children as young as seven were forced into military operations and to commit atrocities. Equally disturbing, finds UNICEF, is that approximately 101,000 children are acting as heads of household, since their parents were murdered, have died of AIDS, or are in prison. UNICEF is working to help these children recapture some elements of a normal life.

On 7 April, 2004, the International Day of Reflection on the Genocide in Rwanda, millions will observe a moment of silence to remember the victims.

As the world remembers the ten-year anniversary of the genocide in Rwanda, the country's children continue to live with the devastating effects of this brutal conflict.

When the genocide ended in 1994, 800,000 people had been murdered—300,000 of these victims were children. In addition, 95,000 children had been orphaned.

Almost All Rwandan Children Were Victims

Virtually all of Rwandan children witnessed unspeakable horror. Thousands of children were victims of brutality and rape, and thousands of children—some as young as seven—were forced into military operations and forced to commit violent acts against their will.

"The children of Rwanda witnessed unspeakable violence," said UNICEF Executive Director Carol Bellamy. "Tens of thousands lost their mothers and fathers. Thousands were victims of horrific brutality and rape. The impact of the tragedy simply cannot be overstated."

Thousands of Children Are Heads of Household

Ten years later, the children of Rwanda are still suffering from the consequences of a conflict created exclusively by adults.

There are an estimated 101,000 children that are heading approximately 42,000 households. These children have lost parents for various reasons—many were murdered during the genocide, some have died from AIDS and others are in prison for genocide-related crimes.

Helping Children Reclaim Their Lives

UNICEF and its partners are helping a generation of Rwandan children reclaim their lives, especially in the areas of health, counselling and education:

- offering support of child-headed households by providing children with school materials, counselling, income-generating activities and vocational training
- preventing the spread of HIV/AIDS through education and counselling
- providing immunization, and
- providing support for the regular school system and helping children outside of the school system.

Children Forced to Join the Military

Thousands of children—some younger than seven years old—were forced to join military operations during the conflict and forced to commit atrocities against their will. Not only do these children suffer emotional trauma from their experiences, many of them were imprisoned after the genocide.

"We are still accountable for supporting reconciliation and healing, and for ensuring that such atrocities never happen again," said Bellamy. "'Never again' means holding perpetrators accountable and restoring the dignity by commemorating or alleviating their suffering."

Young Cambodians Who Survived Genocide Can Identify with Anne Frank's Story

Tibor Krausz

Tibor Krausz is a correspondent for the Christian Science Monitor *and frequently writes about issues and people of the Asian region of the world.*

A young Cambodian woman who hid from the ongoing civil war between the Khmer Rouge guerillas and government forces in the early 1990s discovered Anne Frank's story a decade after the mass murder conducted in her country. After earning her master's degree and visiting Holocaust memorials and death camps, she obtained permission to translate Frank's diary into Khmer, her native language. According to Krausz in the following selection, the message of Frank's diary struck a chord with other young Cambodians who had survived genocide. According to the Documentation Center of Cambodia, it also inspired some Cambodian students to chronicle their own experiences. The book is also being translated for Laotian children.

As a young girl in the early 1990s, Sayana Ser often spent the night cowering in fear with her family in an underground shelter her father had dug beneath their home on the outskirts of this capital city [Phnom Penh].

Outside, marauding bands of Khmer Rouge guerrillas battled it out with government forces. Meanwhile, brutal mass murder was still fresh on civilians' minds.

Tibor Krausz, "Anne Frank Diary Resonates with Cambodians," *Jewish Journal*, October 6, 2008. Reproduced by permission.

A decade later, as a 19-year-old scholarship student in the Netherlands, Sayana chanced upon the memoirs of another girl who had feared for her life in even more dire circumstances.

Sayana Discovers Anne Frank's Story

It was *The Diary of a Young Girl* by Anne Frank, the precocious Jewish teenager who hid from the Nazis in occupied Amsterdam until her family's hiding place was discovered and she was sent to her death in the Bergen-Belsen concentration camp.

"While reading the book I couldn't hold my tears back," Sayana recalls. "I wondered how Anna must have felt and how she could bear it."

Sayana now is the director of a student outreach and educational program at a Cambodian research institution that documents the Khmer Rouge genocide. Between 1975 and 1979, up to 2 million people—a fourth of the population—perished on [Khmer Rouge leader] Pol Pot's "killing fields" in one of the worst mass murders since the Holocaust.

Sayana, who wrote her master's thesis about "dark tourism," or touristic voyeurism at genocide sites in Cambodia and elsewhere, also visited several Holocaust memorials and death camps.

"I couldn't believe how one human being could do this to another, whether they were Jews or Khmers," she says.

Translating the Diary into Khmer

On returning home, she sought permission to translate the Anne Frank diary into Khmer.

The Holocaust classic was published by the country's leading genocide research group, the Documentation Center of Cambodia. It is now available for Khmer students at high school libraries in Phnom Penh alongside locally written books about the Khmer Rouge period. Such books include *First They*

Chim Math, a Cambodian survivor of Pol Pot's vicious Khmer Rouge regime, visits the Tuol Sleng Genocide Museum in Phnom Penh in 2007. The Documentation Center of Cambodia notes that young Cambodians used Anne Frank's diary as a source of inspiration and comfort under the Khmer Rouge. © Mak Remissa/EPA/Corbis.

Killed My Father by Loung Ung, which recounts the harrowing experiences of a child survivor of the killing fields.

"I have seen many Anna Franks in Cambodia," says Youk Chhang, the head of the documentation center and Cambodia's foremost researcher on genocide.

A child survivor himself, Chhang lost siblings and numerous relatives in the mass murders perpetrated by Pol Pot and his followers.

"If we Cambodians had read her diary a long time ago," he says, "perhaps there could have been a way for us to prevent the Cambodian genocide from happening."

The Diary Remains Relevant

Anne Frank's message, he adds, remains as potent as ever.

"Genocide continues to happen in the world around us even today," Youk says. "Her diary can still play an important role in prevention."

Although the story of Anne and her resilient optimism in the face of murderous evil has touched millions of readers around the world, it may particularly resonate with Cambodians, Sayana adds.

"Under Pol Pot, many children were separated from their families. They faced starvation and were sent to the front to fight and die," she explains. "Like Anna, they never knew peace and the warmth of a home."

Diary Inspires Young Cambodians

Inspired by Anne's diary, she adds, some Cambodian students have begun to write their own diaries to chronicle the sorrows and joys of their daily lives.

Children in Laos, too, can soon learn of Anne's story and insights.

In the impoverished, war-torn communist country bordering Cambodia, almost a million people perished during the Vietnam War, while countless landmines and a low-level insurgency continue to take lives daily.

Yet with books for children almost nonexistent beyond simple school textbooks, Lao students remain largely ignorant of the world and history. In a private initiative, an American expat[riate] publisher is now bringing them children's classics translated into Lao, including Anne Frank's diary.

"I was describing the book to a bright college graduate here and gave him a little context," says Sasha Alyson, the founder of Big Brother House, a small publishing house in Vientiane, the Lao capital, which specializes in books for Lao children. He recalls the student asking "World War II? Is that the same as Star Wars?"

Anna Frank's *Diary of a Young Girl*, he says, will provide Lao children with a much-needed lesson in history.

For Further Discussion

1. Carol Ann Lee (Chapter 1) and Nigel A. Caplan (Chapter 2) state that Anne's diary reveals the promise of a writer whose talent would likely have been recognized later in life had she survived the Holocaust. Do you think Anne was a good writer? If so, what aspects of her writing lead you to that conclusion? If you do not think she was a good writer, what components of her writing do you find lacking?

2. Several of the selections in this book, including those of Judith Goldstein, Lawrence Langer, and Alvin H. Rosenfeld (Chapter 2), assert that Anne Frank's diary promoted a sentimentalized view of genocide and the Holocaust, since it does not address how Anne died. Further, state these authors, the diary is not representative of Jews' experience in that era. Did these selections challenge your assumptions and beliefs about Anne and her diary? Based on your own reading and knowledge, do you think you have a realistic view of genocide, the Holocaust, and how Jews were treated by the Nazis?

3. Felix Padel and Samarendra Das, as well as Bruce Fein and Rosie Malek-Yonan (Chapter 3), describe genocide that is occurring in the present day. As horrific as they are, do you think these situations qualify as genocide, given the backdrop of the Holocaust and the scope of the Nazis' program to obliterate Jews from the face of the earth? Does genocide have only one definition, or can it take many forms?

4. In Chapter 3, Ronald Elly Wanda promotes the opinion that international criminal justice systems are ineffective in prosecuting genocide in the twenty-first century. With

all of the media attention and access to information about these atrocities, why do you think they continue to occur? What should the international community do to prevent genocide and prosecute its perpetrators?

For Further Reading

Rachel Feldhay Brenner, *Writing as Resistance: Four Women Confronting the Holocaust*. University Park: Pennsylvania State University Press, 1997.

Anne Frank, *Het Achterhuis*. Foreword by Annie Romein-Verschoor. Amsterdam: Contact, 1947.

———, *Anne Frank: The Diary of a Young Girl*. Trans. B.M. Mooyaart-Doubleday. Introduction by Eleanor Roosevelt. Garden City, NY: Doubleday, 1952; with new preface by George Stevens, New York: Pocket Books, 1958.

———, *Anne Frank: The Diary of a Young Girl*. New York: Washington Square Press, 1963; reprinted as *The Diary of Anne Frank*. Foreword by Storm Jameson. Illustrations by Elisabeth Trimby. London: Heron Books, 1973.

———, *Anne Frank's Tales from the Secret Annex*. Portions previously published in *The Works of Anne Frank* and *Tales from the House Behind*, with translations from the original manuscript, *Verhaaltjes en gebeurtenissen uit het Achterhuis*, by Ralph Manheim and Michel Mok. Garden City, NY: Doubleday, 1983.

———, *The Diary of Anne Frank: The Critical Edition*. Ed. by David Barnouw and Gerrold van der Stroom. Trans. Arnold J. Pomerans and B.M. Mooyaart-Doubleday. Introduction by Harry Paape, Gerrold van der Stroom, and David Barnouw. Garden City, NY: Doubleday, 1989.

———, *The Diary of Anne Frank: The Definitive Edition*. Ed. Otto Frank and Miriam Pressler. New York: Doubleday, 1995.

———, *Tales from the House Behind: Fables, Personal Reminiscences, and Short Stories*. Translation from the original Dutch manuscript, *Verhalen rondom het achter-*

huis, by H.H.B. Mosberg and Michel Mok. Kingswood, England: World's Work, 1962.

————, *The Works of Anne Frank*. Introduction by Ann Birstein and Alfred Kazin. Garden City, NY: Doubleday, 1959.

John Hersey, *The Wall*. New York: Knopf, 1950.

Jacqueline van Maarsen, *My Friend Anne Frank*. New York: Vantage Press, 1996.

Dalia Ofer and Lenore J. Weitzman, *Women in the Holocaust*. New Haven, CT: Yale University Press, 1998.

Elie Wiesel, *Night*. New York: Hill & Wang, 1960.

Bibliography

Books

Chaya Brasz   *Removing the Yellow Badge: The Struggle for a Jewish Community in the Postwar Netherlands.* Jerusalem: Institute for Research on Dutch Jewry, 1996.

G. Jan Colijin and Marcia S. Littell, eds.   *The Netherlands and Nazi Genocide.* New York: Edwin Mellen Press, 1992.

Margaret Randolph Higonnet, Jane Jenson, Sonya Michel, and Margaret Collins Weitz   *Behind the Lines: Gender and the Two World Wars.* New Haven, CT: Yale University Press, 1987.

Lawrence L. Langer   *Using and Abusing the Holocaust.* Bloomington and Indianapolis: Indiana University Press, 2006.

Carol Ann Lee   *Anne Frank and the Children of the Holocaust.* New York: Viking, 2006.

Ralph Melnick   *The Stolen Legacy of Anne Frank: Meyer Levin, Lillian Hellman, and the Staging of the Diary.* New Haven, CT: Yale University Press, 1997.

Menno Metselaar, Ruud van der Rol, Arnold Pomerans, and Anne Frank Stichting
Anne Frank: Her Life in Words and Pictures from the Archives of the Anne Frank House. New York: Roaring Brook Press, 2009.

Miriam Pressler
The Story of Anne Frank. London: Macmillan, 1999.

Francine Prose
Anne Frank: The Book, the Life, the Afterlife. New York: HarperCollins, 2009.

Susan Goldman Rubin and Bill Farnsworth
The Anne Frank Case: Simon Wiesenthal's Search for the Truth. New York: Holiday House, 2009.

Ernst Schnabel
The Footsteps of Anne Frank. London: Pan Books, 1976.

Tzvetan Todorov
Facing the Extreme: Moral Life in the Concentration Camps. London: Phoenix, 2000.

Simon Wiesenthal
Justice Not Vengeance. London: Weidenfeld & Nicholson, 1989.

Cara Wilson
Love, Otto: The Legacy of Anne Frank. Kansas City, MO: Andrews and McMeel, 1995.

Robert S. Wistrich
Anti-Semitism: The Longest Hatred. London: Methuen, 1991.

Periodicals

Rosemary Black "Anne Frank Told Fairy Tales to Children in Concentration Camp, Says Survivor," *New York Daily News*, March 22, 2010.

Barbara Brotman "Anne Frank Photos Show Cheerful Life Before the War," *Chicago Tribune*, March 29, 2010.

Otto Frank "Has Germany Forgotten Anne Frank?" *Coronet*, February 1960.

Nancy Franklin "The Diary of Anne Frank," *New Yorker*, December 15, 1997.

M. Gerstenfeld "Dead Jews and Living Trees," *Jerusalem Post*, August 28, 2010.

Sylvia Patterson Iskander "Anne Frank's Autobiographical Style," *Children's Literature Association Quarterly*, Summer 1991.

Thomas Larson "'In Spite of Everything': The Definitive Indefinite Anne Frank," *Antioch Review*, Winter 2000.

Meyer Levin "The Suppressed Anne Frank," *Jewish Week*, August 31, 1980.

Jacob B. Michaelson "Remembering Anne Frank," *Judaism*, Spring 1997.

Cynthia Ozick "Who Owns Anne Frank?" *New Yorker*, October 6, 1997.

Carol Roach

"The Life and Death of Anne Frank: Montreal Betrayal of Anne Frank," *Montreal Health Examiner*, October 2010.

Alvin H. Rosenfeld

"The Americanization of the Holocaust," *Commentary*, June 1995.

Robert Sackett

"Memory by Way of Anne Frank: Enlightenment and Denial Among West Germans, Circa 1960," *Holocaust and Genocide Studies*, Fall 2002.

Eva Schloss

"The Agony of Otto Frank," *Time*, June 14, 1999.

Index